Wall Street's Financing of World War I; Liberty Loans and Financial Demonization.

Kerry Segrave

Published by Historical Press, 2023.

WALL STREET'S FINANCING OF WORLD WAR I; LIBERTY LOANS AND FINANCIAL DEMONIZATION.

First edition. March 1, 2023.

Copyright © 2023 Kerry Segrave.

ISBN: 978-1777037086

Written by Kerry Segrave.

Table of Contents

Introduction.

This book examines how the capitalist class financed World War I, specifically the Liberty Loan campaigns, to persuade and compel the underclass to pay a disproportionate share of the cost of that conflict.

Initially, the capitalist class organized the National Security League in 1914 to promote the war, America's entry into it, and to convince the public that the war was necessary. The League also softened the ordinary citizens by preaching themes of preparedness, patriotism, loyalty, and so on. War was in the interest of the capitalist class as it made enormous fortunes for many of them and greatly enriched that class as a whole. However, they did not want to pay the entire cost of that war, so they launched the financial instruments, so-called Liberty Loan campaigns, to convince the public it had a duty to purchase these securities. Those bond campaigns numbered five in total. Two of the drives were in 1917, in the spring and fall, with the official campaigns being of relatively short duration, about a month each. Two more campaigns were held in 1918, again in the spring and fall. A final one was launched in 1919 in the spring, many months after the war had ceased. That last drive was officially called a Victory Loan. Still, the campaigns became known as Liberty Loans One through Five unofficially.

Selling pressure was intense and involved carrots in the form of such things as honor rolls and honor flags. On the other hand, the stick approach was also a dominant campaign feature. The Wall Street crowd used the term "slacker" to refer to anyone who did not buy those securities, which all carried an interest rate slightly below the going rate of interest paid by savings banks.

This book is mainly about the creation of the "financial slacker" by Wall Street and the demonization of slackers, many of whom were subjected to brutality and harsh treatment. People were summarily fired, tarred and feathered, and ridden out of town on a rail. If the

slacker was luckier, he was simply hounded and harassed by bond
soliciting group after group and perhaps named and shamed.

Quotas were set as to the number of bonds to be purchased.
Those quotas were set for Federal Reserve districts, states, counties,
cities, townships, industrial plants, and individuals. And resisters
or refusers were harshly dealt with; no dissent or deviations was
tolerated.

Chapter one examines the way the capitalist class decided to
finance the war. Three options were considered; printing money,
taxation, and borrowing. The first method was quickly dismissed.
Taxes were raised in some cases, and new taxes were implemented
in other cases. However, borrowing was finally selected, paying for
two-thirds of the war costs while taxation accounted for the other
one-third. What was not even considered by the ruling class was
the implementation of some sort of wealth tax. When taxation was
discussed, it was limited to incomes and new taxes such as levies
imposed on chewing gum and an amusement tax. Yet the vast wealth
of the ruling class lay in its assets and property, and so on, not in
the income that was listed on a tax form. Wealth was much more
important to the capitalist class than income, which comprised only
a tiny portion of overall wealth. Figures from the ear showed the
capitalists could have paid for the entire war with only a minor
wealth drawdown. The amount of money that class had lying inactive
in the banking system would have been almost enough to pay the
total cost.

In chapter two, the way of selling the bonds to the public and
the intense use of advertising is examined. Celebrities such as Charlie
Chaplin, Mary Pickford, and Douglas Fairbanks, among many
others, donated their time and efforts to selling bonds. At the other
end of the scale were the Four-Minute Men, also volunteers, who
went anywhere in the community they were sent to and orated, for
four minutes, on any topic selected for them by the US Treasury

Department; topics such as patriotism, Americanism, and, of course, the Liberty Loan drives.

Chapter three looks at the editorials, opinions, attitudes, and threats made by community opinion makers. They were uniformly in favor of the bond program and just as rabidly against the financial slacker. It is possible that many of these pronouncements from the opinion makers led to much of the violence that was often meted out to those who refused to buy and those who bought less than they should have purchased, by standards set by others and not known to the victims.

Commercial tie-ins were popular as various retailers and manufacturers tried to merge Liberty bond hype with their advertising material. While pitching his toothpaste, one manufacturer worked material into his ad urging readers to buy his toothpaste and some bonds; the fountain pen maker wanted people to use his instrument when they signed up for bonds. That topic is examined in chapter four.

In many cases, those who refused to purchase bonds were subject to intense investigations by others in the community. It seemed apparent that members of various investigation committees obtained financial records that should have remained private. That is the topic of chapter five.

Chapters six and seven look at the more brutal side of the bond programs. The attacks launched on refusers and resisters used naming and shaming. If those methods failed, they moved into more aggressive and physical methods – coercion and force.

Chapter 1. How to Finance a War.

When the United States of America declared war on the German empire on April 6, 1917, it officially entered a conflict that had begun in Europe on July 28, 1914. One of the first orders of business was to decide how to finance the war. The United States Treasury and the Federal Reserve Bank united under William Gibbs McAdoo as the leader of both institutions to work together to finance World War I. "Any great war must necessarily be a popular movement. It is a kind of a crusade; and like all crusades; it sweeps along on a Powerful stream of romanticism," explained McAdoo. The Federal Reserve System was established in 1914, the year World War I began. During the three years before America entered the conflict, the Federal Reserve had completed its organization and was positioned to play a vital role in the war effort. Richard Sutch wrote the official history of Liberty Bonds that appeared on the Federal Reserve website. He write, "Wars are expensive and, like every governmental effort, they have to be financed through some combination off taxation, borrowing and finally, through the expedience of printing money. For this war, the federal government relied on a mix of one-third new taxes and two-thirds borrowing from the general public. Very little new money was created. The borrowing effort was called the 'Liberty Loan' and was made operational through the sale of Liberty Bonds. These securities were issued by the Treasury, but the Federal Reserve and its member banks conducted the bond sales." With the Treasury and the Federal Reserve united under McAdoo, the two agencies worked together in both the creation of the war plan and its execution. Created was a seven-member Federal Reserve Board, based in Washington D. C., with the Secretary of the Treasury designated ex officio as chairman. The other members were the comptroller of the currency and five members appointed by the US president and confirmed by the Senate. When the United States entered the war, it became apparent that an "unprecedented effort" would be required to divert the nation's industrial capacity away from meeting consumer demand toward fulfilling the needs of the military. At the time of the declaration of war, the American economy was "operating at full capacity," so war effort needs could not be met by putting underutilized resources to work; "The wartime population would have to sacrifice to pay the bill, and McAdoo understood the point." Said McAdoo, shortly after the United States declared war: "We must be willing to give up something of personal convenience, something of personal comfort, something of our treasure – all, if necessary, and our lives in the bargain, to support our noble sons who go out to die for us."[1]

While there were three ways to finance a war – taxation, borrowing, and printing money – for McAdoo, printing money was off the table as a method from the beginning. He worried that printing money would generate inflation, as happened with the issuing of the "greenback" during the Civil War. McAdoo also opposed printing money because he thought it would hide war costs rather than keep the public "engaged and committed." So, he chose a mix of taxation and borrowing by selling war bonds. Originally the idea was to finance the war with an equal division between taxation and borrowing, with each method used to produce 50 percent of the financing. Taxation worked to reduce consumption (people had less money to spend). Another advantage was that Congress could set the taxation rate schedule to target those they thought should bear the most significant burden. United States President Woodrow Wilson and the Democrats in Congress wanted a progressive tax rate schedule. The highest marginal rate eventually reached 77 percent on incomes over $1 million. McAdoo resisted any efforts to raise a higher proportion of the costs from taxation, deciding that taxation had reached its "acceptable" limit. Thus the revised goal was to raise one-third of the war cost from taxes and two-thirds from borrowing.

Financing a war by borrowing need not be inflationary if the public diverted income away from consumption to purchase bonds, went the reasoning. Higher savings as a share of income would necessarily mean lower consumption. Such a change in saving behavior, it was granted, would be challenging to engineer. One question that arose concerning borrowing was where to set the interest rate that would be paid on the war bonds. McAdoo opposed offering high-interest rates (compared to the going rate for comparable securities) because he saw it as a sign of weakness and that it would reward the rich – the very group the income tax was designed to target. He chose to keep interest rates for the Liberty bonds competitive with the current return on comparable assets. Many in the financial community worried that a sale of such a large size was a gamble, and they were unanimous in worrying the bonds might not sell without the promise of an "extra-attractive" return. Also, it was pointed out only a few Americans had any direct knowledge about bonds, and fewer still owned any. [Note that raising money through taxation was restricted to a limited target, namely a tax on incomes. Most of the wealthy class had far more of their assets, and derived income, from other assets besides income. For example, the money held in America in bank deposits alone was enough to pay for the war many times. And the wealthy class then, as now, controlled some 90 percent of those deposits in the hands of about 10 percent of the population. That is, it was never necessary to borrow a dime to finance the war].[2]

At this point, McAdoo conceived of the Liberty Loan plan, a plan with three elements. In the first instance, the public was to be educated about bonds, the causes and objectives of the war, and the financial situation of the nation. McAdoo chose to call the securities "Liberty Bonds" as part of that educational effort. In the second instance, the government would appeal to patriotism and ask everyone – from school children to millionaires – to do their part by reducing consumption and purchasing bonds. In the third instance,

the entire effort would rely upon volunteer labor, thereby avoiding
the money market, brokerage commissions, or a paid sales force. The
Federal Reserve banks would coordinate and manage sales, while the
bonds could be bought at any bank member of the Federal Reserve
System. During the campaign, purchasers of bonds were given
buttons to wear on their clothing and window stickers to display
from their homes, "thus advertising their patriotism." One
acknowledged risk of the plan was that poor sales would signify
weak and insufficient patriotism. To avoid a failure of the entire bond
issue, the government arranged to sell them in a series of brief but
intense subscription campaigns. The first campaign was announced
on April 28, 1917, 22 days after America formally declared war. That
first bond offering had a target of $2 billion in sales and carried
a 3.5 percent interest rate. That was slightly below the rate paid
by savings banks on customer deposits (3.5% to 4.0%) or the yield
on high-grade municipal bonds (3.9% to 4.2%). The rate was
deliberately set slightly below prevailing rates for similar investments
because there was a fear that people with savings accounts or
municipal bond holdings would use those funds to purchase Liberty
bonds if the Liberty bond interest rate was higher than what was
paid by a savings account. In that case, there would have been no
increased savings or reduced consumption – only a rearrangement of
assets within a person's portfolio. McAdoo also knew that financial
institutions would strongly resist competition for their deposit
money, that is, competition from the government. The bonds
themselves were negotiable, with interest coupons cashable every
six months. The term for those bonds was 30 years, but they were
callable after 15 years. The lowest denomination bond available for
purchase was $50. Some thought that would put the bonds out
of the reach of the general public. At that time, a manufacturing
plant worker's average pay was about 35 cents an hour. Thus a $50
bond would take two to three weeks of wages. However, officials

opposed any lower denominations due to the administrative costs of tracking ownership, and that was also why the government issued the bonds as bearer instruments. Had bearer bonds been issued in small denominations, they could have been used like currency, thus defeating McAdoo's reason for refusing to print money. They would be used like money to buy items and keep consumption up.[3]

McAdoo found another way to make his war bonds affordable. He introduced an installment plan so even the poorest could purchase Thrift Stamps. They cost only 25 cents and were labeled by the Treasury Department "little baby bonds." When someone purchased a Thrift stamp, he pasted it on a card until 16 were affixed to the card, at which point they were exchanged for a $5 stamp called a War Savings Stamp. They were affixed to a War Savings Certificate, which also earned interest, as did the Thrift stamps. When 10 of the $5 stamps were collected, the War Savings Certificate could be exchanged for a $50 Liberty bond. Initial fears of poor sales proved utterly unwarranted. The First Loan was oversubscribed by about 50 percent, with more than four million subscribers involved. Nationally, that represented about one out of every six households. Fifty percent of the bonds sold in the First drive were for the lowest face value, $50, while one-third of those sold were for the $100 bond. There were four Liberty Loan drives and a fifth drive called Victory Loan, which took place after the armistice in April 1919. The Second Liberty Loan drive was open for six weeks, concluding on November 15, 1917, and raising $3 billion. Drives three and four took place in 1918, and each lasted officially for about one month; the April drive raised $3 billion, while the October campaign raised $6 billion. Because rates on alternative investments had risen, the rates on the subsequent loans were increased to keep them competitive. Interest on the Second loan was 4.0%, while it was 4.25 % on both the Third and Fourth drives. Purchasers of the First bond issue and later the Second issue could exchange their bonds for the later, higher-yielding bonds. All five loan campaigns were oversubscribed.[4]

The loan drives were the subject of what Sutch described as "the greatest advertising effort ever conducted." That First drive used 11,000 billboards and placed streetcar ads in 3,200 cities. All of that space was donated and cost the Liberty Loan authorities not one cent. During the second drive, 60,000 women were recruited to sell bonds. That volunteer army stationed women at factory gates to distribute seven million flyers on a day designated as "Liberty Day." The mail-order houses of Montgomery Ward and Sears-Roebuck mailed two million information sheets to farm women. Libraries inserted 4.5 million Liberty Loan reminder cards in public libraries in 1,500 libraries. Celebrities, such as Charlie Chaplin, Mary Pickford, and Douglas Fairbanks, among the most famous celebrities in the United States, toured the nation, holding bond rallies attended by thousands. All that effort came from a home-grown propaganda ministry called the Committee on Public Information. That propaganda effort was essential not only to sell the bonds but also to sell the war. Public sentiment before 1917 was not only against American involvement in the war but was not even united on which European military to favor. Running for re-election in 1916 as President of the United States, one of Woodrow Wilson's slogans was, "He kept us out of war." Wilson's Republican opponent, Charles Evans Hughes, was also against the war. For the task of molding public opinion, Wilson turned to an investigative journalist named George Creel, who staffed the Committee on Public Information with psychologists, journalists, artists, and admen. The committee appealed to "innate" motives such as competition (which city would buy the most bonds, which would achieve the greatest oversubscription level, which county or state would beat which other county or state, and so forth); the familial (my father bought bonds, did yours); guilt (if you can't enlist you must do something – so invest); fear (keep the enemy from reaching our shores); revenge (get even with the Kaiser); social image (wear your bond button to show you conform); gregariousness (we are all in this together); the impulse to follow the leader (Wilson and McAdoo were both publicly lauded for having personally bought bonds); the herd instinct, and so forth.[5]

By the end of the war, after four drives, 20 million individuals had purchased bonds. There were then only 24 million households in America. More than $17 billion had been raised; in addition, the extra taxes collected amounted to $8.8 billion. Almost two-thirds of the war funding came from bonds and one-third from taxes. Most of McAdoo's bonds were bought by the public, 62 percent of the value sold, by one estimate. A government survey of almost 13,000 urban wage-earners conducted in 1918 and 1919 indicated that 68 percent owned Liberty bonds. Consumption, as a percentage of personal income, fell during the war by about 10 percent. Along with the personal income tax was an increase in the corporate income tax, an entirely new "excess profits tax," and excise taxes on such "luxuries" as cars, motorcycles, pleasure boats, musical instruments, talking machines, picture frames, jewelry, cameras, riding habits, playing cards, perfumes, cosmetics, silk stockings, proprietary medicines, candy, and chewing gum. These ranged from (ad valorem tax) three percent on chewing gum and toilet soap to 100 percent on brass knuckles and double-edged dirk knives. A graduated estate tax exempted the first $50,000 and rose progressively from one percent to 25 percent on amounts over $10,050,000. Also, a variety of miscellaneous war taxes were introduced. These included taxes on transportation services, admission to places of entertainment, social, athletic, and sporting club dues, a stamp tax on legal documents, a tax on the value of the outstanding corporate stock, and a tax on the use of yachts.[6]

The above was taken from the Federal Reserve's official website. While the facts may be more or less accurate, the interpretations were likely biased to a greater or lesser degree. Slightly different information came from the Wikipedia page for Liberty bonds. That page noted that the Act of Congress that authorized the Liberty bond was still used today as the authority under which all United States Treasury bonds are issued. The First bond drive was issued on April 24, 1917, and authorized $1.9 billion in bonds at 3.5 percent. On October 1, 1917, the Second Liberty Loan offered $3.8 billion in bonds with an interest rate of 4.0 percent. On April 5, 1918, the Third loan offered $4.1 billion at an interest rate of 4.15 percent. The Fourth loan was issued on September 28, 1918, and offered $6.9 billion in bonds with an interest rate of 4.25 percent. That First issue had a maturity date of 30 years but was callable after 15 years; it raised $2 billion with 5.5 million people purchasing bonds. The Second issue had a 25-year maturity date but was callable after ten years. In total, $3.8 billion was raised from sales, with 9.4 million people purchasing bonds. According to this account, the response to the First issue was "unenthusiastic." Although the issue reportedly sold out, it probably had to be done below par because the notes traded on the resale market at below par. That is, buying a $100 bond for less than $100 effectively increased the interest rate received by the discount buyer. One reaction to the rumors of below-par sales was to attack bond traders as "unpatriotic" if they sold below par. The New York Stock Exchange Board of Governors investigated brokerage firms that sold below par to determine if "pro-German influences" were at work. The board reportedly forced one such broker to repurchase the bonds at par and make a $100,000 donation to the Red Cross [*The Financier*, June 23, 1917, p.1741]. Such weaknesses continued with the 4.25 percent issue being priced as low as 94 cents on the dollar upon issue. McAdoo responded with an aggressive campaign to popularize the bonds. He used a division of

the Committee on Public Information called the Four Minute Men
to help sell Liberty bonds and Thrift stamps. Also, famous celebrities
were used to sell the securities by, for example, hosting bond rallies.
Among the celebrities, besides those mentioned above, were Elsie
Janis and Al Jolson. Chaplin also made a short film, *The Bond*, at
his own expense for the drive. During the Third Liberty Loan, nine
million posters, five million window stickers, and 10 million bond
buttons were produced and distributed. The Fourth loan was issued
on October 24, 1918, paid 4.25 percent in interest, and was callable
starting 15 years later, in 1933. Its maturity date was 1938. Originally
$6 billion was tendered, and about $7 billion was sold.[7]

Peak US indebtedness for these wartime financial instruments
of Liberty bonds, Victory bonds, War Savings Stamps, War Savings
Certificates, and so forth, was reached in August 1919 when that
debt total reached $25,596,000,000. Through selling Liberty bonds,
the government raised around $17 billion for the war effort.
Considering there were roughly 100 million Americans during that
time, each American, on average, spent about $1,700 on Liberty
bonds. The Victory (Liberty) Loan was issued on April 21, 1919,
to a value of $4.5 billion at an interest rate of 4.75 percent; they
matured after four years and were callable after three years. The first
three issues and the Victory issue were partially retired during the
1920s; most of these bonds were simply re-financed through other
government securities. In 1927, the Second and Third issues,
together worth $5 billion, were called for redemption and
refinanced through the issuance of other government securities
through the Treasury Department. Some of the principal was retired.
For example, of the $3.1 billion owed on the Second issue, $575
million in principal was retired, with the remainder being
refinanced. The majority of the Fourth issue was still outstanding
in the 1930s; it paid a higher interest rate, and many holders of
earlier issues had rolled their holdings over into the Fourth, which

remained an option. The amounts initially tendered for the five issues were, respectively, $5 billion, $3 billion, $3 billion, $6 billion, and $4.5 billion.[8]

Victory bonds could be bought with 10 percent down, and the balance paid off monthly, usually over the six following months. A second option was to borrow the money from the bank and buy the bond outright. However, the bank changed interest on those loans at a rate of 6.0 percent, compared to the 4.75 percent interest earned from the Victory bonds.[9]

That method of financing contradicted the supposed arrangement for issues one through four of the Liberty Loans. For example, articles that appeared around the same time, the beginning of October 1918, in a Pennsylvania newspaper and a Kentucky publication, indicated that all the banks in those areas had made arrangements whereby they would lend Liberty bond purchasers money for the purchase of bonds at a rate of 4.25 percent interest – the same rate as paid by the Fourth issue of bonds. Any bond thus purchased was held by the bank as collateral, although the purchaser was allowed to clip the interest coupons as they became due. The period for which the money was lent was 90 days, but the loan could be extended at the same interest rate at the end of the 90 days if necessary.[10]

An advertisement in a Texas newspaper in June 1917, at the end of the First issue, illustrated clearly the difficulties involved in getting people to buy Liberty bonds. An article that urged slackers to buy bonds argued for the positive aspects of the bonds, pointing out, for one thing, that the bonds paid 3.25 percent interest. Just one column over on the same page was an ad for a bank in the city. That ad remarked that it paid 4.0 percent on savings accounts.[11]

Even then, in June 1917, the term "slacker" was in general use and no longer warranted appearing in quotation marks as new terms usually did during their early appearances in print. However, the word "slacker" was considered new in the American vocabulary just a year earlier, in April 1916. It was not new, though, in England, where it had been used for years and meant one who shirked. For example, around universities in England, one who got up late, lolled around in his room, and did nothing was a "slacker." And the boy who refused to go out for sports and help his college was also a slacker. It was used in England as a term of reproach, and the fear of being called one was said to be a good motivator to cause one to change his behavior. So when the war began in England and volunteers were asked to come forward, the man who refused to volunteer without a good reason was a slacker. It continued to be used that way in England and referred to a draft dodger or a financial tightwad. It quickly transferred to America with the same meaning and usage. Said a journalist; "It is the lax fellows, the 'slackers' who are the parasites on society."[12]

The place for competitiveness in the bond drives could be seen in the quota systems or in the allotments that were generated from the largest unit, quotas for each of the 12 Federal Reserve districts, down to the smallest unit, quotas for each individual. In between, there were quotas for each state, each county, each city, each township, and so forth. What never appeared in print was the underlying rationale or formula by which the quotas were generated. The population was one obvious consideration, as were total banking deposits for areas. For individual allotments, though, the formula was even more mystifying. Likely much information that should have remained private and confidential was accessed by the various Liberty Loan committees, which existed everywhere. People on these committees were mainly "important" and well-placed men, at least within their area, and thus had more access to information and financial data and the power to obtain it than most citizens would have wanted. For example, Third Liberty Loan quotas in the nation's 12 Federal

Districts were as follows, using the principal city in each district; Boston $250 million; New York $900 million; Philadelphia $250 million; Cleveland $300 million; Richmond $130 million; Atlanta $90 million; Chicago $425 million; St. Louis $130 million; Minneapolis $105 million; Kansas City $130 million; Dallas $80 million; and San Francisco $210 million. That Third loan exceeded $1 billion of its target to hit $4,170,019,650. The number of people purchasing bonds reached over 17 million, one in every six of the nation's population.[13]

Another example of competition infused into the program was the system of honor rolls and honor flags. A reporter noted in April 1918, "The system of honor rolls in each municipality, community or business organization, bearing the names of subscribers, and of honor flags, to be given to each city exceeding its quota, is expected to stimulate the number of subscriptions. This plan will disclose who subscribes and who refuses to buy."[14]

One significant difference between the Liberty bond program and the War Savings Stamps was that in the case of the latter, it was the United States Post Office that played the central role in promoting and distributing the stamps, in contrast with the Liberty Loans, which were distributed primarily through the financial institutions such as banks. Those stamps were often aimed at the "common citizens" and even children. Perhaps it was thought to be a simple way to distribute that product through the network of American post offices, facilities that even children would enter and wherein they felt comfortable.[15]

The idea that the war should be paid for by mostly borrowing was never at issue once the authorities abandoned the idea of a 50:50 split between borrowing and taxation and settled on a split of 66:33 in favor of borrowing. And even some of the money raised through taxation came off the backs of the lower income groups, such as amusement taxes, a tax on chewing gum, and so on. The idea that the war should be financed solely from the immense wealth of the ruling class was never even discussed. An editor writing in April 1918 noted that; "The fact is that the borrowing of money for the war is a necessary government activity in which the people must cooperate....Taxes are levied up to the amount which it is believed wise to collect in that manner, and the rest is demanded as a loan." And, he continued, "The amount that an individual will subscribe to the loan is left to his own judgment – within reasonable limits. This is done in order that the public may be inconvenienced as little as possible. But it is not done in order to permit individuals to shirk their obligations. The obligation of every individual to subscribe to each government loan to the extent of his ability is just as great and just as binding as his obligation to pay the taxes that are levied against him."[16]

An earlier article in May 1917 in a New York City newspaper alluded to the ruling class concerning the loan, but only to state that class could not and should not be expected to pay for the war. It noted firstly that; "Notwithstanding the vigorous efforts of bankers to make the loan a huge success, the public is not responding as it should...Our bankers actually are working at a personal loss to make the loan go with the public and it is the duty of the public..." to subscribe to meet the quotas. Bankers were not working at a loss, and if they were pushing hard to get the public to subscribe, it was because it let their class off the hook with respect to paying for the conflict. Bankers, of course, were benefiting enormously financially from the program – but that did not mean they wanted to or were willing to pay for it. They believed in the old axiom; privatize the profits, socialize the costs. Concluded the newsman, "There is an ample supply of money in the hands of the public to take up the loan on the basis of small subscriptions and it should not be said of the public that it preferred to let Wall Street and the big corporations throughout the country do the financing which in its every essential should be a public affair."[17]

The war profiteering on Wall Street started even before America joined the war. Although, as J. P. Morgan banking firm partner Thomas Lamont noted, when war broke out in Europe in the summer of 1914, "American citizens were urged to remain neutral in action, in word, and even in thought, [but] our firm had never for one moment been neutral; we didn't know how to be. From the very start we did everything we could to contribute to the cause of the Allies." John Pierpont Morgan died in 1913 – before the passage of the Federal Reserve Act he had stewarded into existence, before the outbreak of war in Europe – but the Morgan banking house remained powerful, with the Morgan bank under the direction of John Pierpont Morgan Jr., maintaining its position as America's preeminent financier The Morgan bank signed its first commercial agreement with the British Army Council in January 1915, just four months into the war. That initial contract – a $12 million purchase of horses for the British war effort to be brokered in the United States by the House of Morgan – was only the beginning. By the war's end, the Morgan bank had brokered $3 billion in transactions for the British military, equal to about half of all American supplies sold to the Allies in the entire war. The Morgan firm had similar arrangements with the French, Russian, Italian, and Canadian governments. The Morgan deals were not without risks, at least theoretical risks. If the Allied powers were to lose the war, there could have been financial problems for Morgan. By 1917 the British government's overdraft with Morgan stood at over $400 million. It was not clear they would win the war and be able to repay all their debts when the war was over. However, in April 1917, just eight days after America's formal declaration of war on Germany, the US Congress passed the War Loan Act that extended $1 billion in credit to the Allies. The first $200 million went to the British. That entire amount was immediately handed over to Morgan as partial payment on UK debt to the bank. When, a few days later, $100 million went to the French government, it, too, was immediately returned to Morgan. But the debts continued to mount. In 1917 and 1918, the US treasury – aided by the Pilgrims Society member Benjamin Strong – president of the newly-created Federal Reserve – quietly paid off the Allied powers' war debts to the J. P. Morgan banking firm.[18]

Major General Smedley Butler of the US military penned a now-famous book in 1935 titled *War is a Racket*. In it, he wrote, "In the World War [1] a mere handful garnered the profits of the conflict. At least 21,000 new millionaires were made in the United States during the World War. That many admitted their huge blood gains in their income tax returns. How many other war millionaires falsified their tax returns no one knows." After America entered the war, the good times for Wall Street bankers improved. Bernard Baruch, the powerful financier who led Woodrow Wilson into Democratic party headquarters in New York City, noted a reporter, "like a poodle on a string" to receive his marching orders during the 1912 election, was appointed to head the newly-created "War Industries Board." Through this agency, with war hysteria at its height Baruch and his fellow Wall Street financiers and industrialists were given unprecedented powers over manufacturing and production throughout the American economy, "including the ability to set quotas, fix prices, standardize products, and, as a subsequent congressional investigation showed, pad costs so that the true size of the fortunes that the war profiteers extracted from the blood of the dead soldiers were hidden from the public." Spending government funds at an annual rate of $10 billion, the Board minted many new millionaires in the American economy, such as Samuel Prescott Bush [yes, that Bush family], who happened to sit on the War Industries Board. Baruch himself was said to have personally profited from his position as head of that board to the amount of $200 million.[19]

A report that was published in July 1920, out of New York City, declared that the combined corporations of the nation earned in net profits approximately $4.3 billion more per year during the years 1916 through 1918 than in the corresponding three-year, pre-war period and that those excess profits had cost each family in the United States a total of $1,500 (over one-fifth of their average total income over that period). That report came from W. Jett Lauck, an economist, and statistician. Lauck also showed that 2,030 corporations earned net profits of over 100 percent on their capital stock; 5,724 firms showed net profits of more than 50 percent, and 20,000 concerns earned from 20 percent to 30 percent. Since the armistice, said Lauck, "industries engaged in the production of clothing, food, household supplies and other staple necessities of life have exploited the public to an even greater extent than during the years 1916-17-18..." by some 20 percent more than excessive war profits. Lauck added, "First hand evidence on profiteering is accentuated by the huge undivided profits which are now flowing out in surplus stock dividends following the recent supreme court decision. This indicates that profiteering already revealed is only a fraction of the real extent of profiteering, since profits held in reserve for a favorable moment of distribution." Examples he gave included that meat packers' profits on hides increased 475 percent; tanners' profits 221 percent; the shoe manufacturers' profits 54.2 percent; and the retailers' profits 102.2 percent. Lauck also showed that high prices had not been due to and necessitated by increased labor costs, as the capitalists often argued; "Wage increases have been a result and not a cause of high prices; wage increases have not kept pace with price increases, price increases have been out of all proportion to wage increases, and labor save in isolated instances has not profiteered either during or since the war. Labor increases are

multiplied four or five times by the profiteering in passing them on
to the public. Bituminous coal miners were given a wage increase
of 27 per cent effective April 1. This amounted to 40 cents per ton.
Immediately the price of coal at the pit-heads in the Virginia field
which had been $2.35 and $2.75 was jumped to $4.35 and $4.75 –
an increase exactly five times the added labor cost." In conclusion,
Lauck declared that the discontinuance of regulatory agencies
created by the war left the public entirely at the mercy of organized
capital. Lauck hoped legislation would be enacted to control prices
created by "the orgy of war-time and post-war profit pyramiding."[20]

In a special report released by the Federal Trade Commission
in the spring of 1920, it was revealed that in the first three years
of the war, profits by the big meat packers "doubled, trebled and
quadrupled." The average annual profit of the big five packers –
Armour, Swift, Wilson, Cudahy, and Morris – was $59,500,000
from 1912 through 1914. Those profits averaged $192,000,000
annually from 1915 through 1917.[21]

United States Senator Arthur Capper (Republican, KS) gave a
speech in the Senate in April 1920, declaring, "The United States has
become a robbers roost," as part of his attack on war profiteering. He
said that proof was to be found in the margin of profit. In one year
alone during the war, the gross income of American corporations
rose from $35.33 billion to $84.5 billion. Capper stated, "Wall
Street's melon patches continued to be warmed by the sun of
privilege, fertilized by the perspiration of labor and watered by the
tears of poverty, and this year will raise a record breaking crop from
the blight of income taxes, while the people are being urged to buy
their coal early and be robbed for less, to abstain from steak one day
a week and to purchase war savings stamps that the United States
may live in nine billion style on a six billion income." The Standard
Oil Company of Indiana had recently increased its capital from $1
million to $30 million, giving its stockholders a stock dividend of

2,900 percent. That partly evolved from that recent US Supreme Court decision in which that body declared stock dividends not taxable. The National Candy Company earnings in 1919 were up 545 percent over 1915. Burns Brothers, the largest retail coal dealer in the United States, made a profit of 40 cents a ton against 23.5 cents three years earlier, in 1916. Said Capper; "These patriotic melon farmers who have made their millions and billions during and since the war now are urging that the soldiers' bonus be raised by a one percent tax on sales to be paid on every dollar spent by every man, woman and child in the United States." Capper favored taking the necessary funds for the soldiers' bonus directly from the profiteers. Senator Irvine Lenroot (Republican, WI), remarked that if a single millionaire were sent to prison "under the laws now on the books some of this profiteering would be stopped."[22]

In urging the United States Congress to pass legislation for the soldiers' bonus, Senator Key Pittman of Nevada (Dem.) reminded his colleagues, from the floor of the Senate, of the vast war profits made by men who were then opposing the bonus. Said Pittman; "When I think of the $10,000,000,000 made in excess profits by the profiteers of this country; when I think of the $15,000,000,000 of profits in addition to the excess profits which were turned by corporations into capital stock for the purpose of avoiding paying of taxes, I am astonished at the greed, the heartlessness and the lack of patriotism of the great financiers of this country" He observed that the bonus could be fully paid with about $1.5 billion – just one-sixth of the excess profits of $10 billion.[23]

A report published in 1922 showed that; "despite stupendous profits and extra charges, war contractors were paid an additional $3,000,000,000 because the armistice ended the possibility of more profits." The railroads were paid more than $700,000,000 for damages done their property while under government control that was necessary to win the war." Also noted was that taxes on large incomes had been reduced to the amount of $90 million annually.[24]

The war was financially very beneficial to the capitalist class, the class that fomented the war in the first place. And that brought up the question of the cost of the war. One report from April 1918, about 3.5 years after World War I officially started, stated the conflict had caused an increase of $111.7 billion in public debt of the 12 leading warring nations, according to tabulations made by the Federal Reserve Board. Of that total, $72.4 billion represented the debt increase of the Allied nations and $39.3 billion that of the other side, the "Central nations." The United States debt incurred since it entered the war was given as $6.55 billion through January 1, 1918.[25]

A later report, long after the war was over, gave the following breakdown of the costs of the war, in dollars in 1914-1918. The total cost to the Central Powers was as follows; Germany $37,775,000,000, Austria-Hungary $20,622,960,000, Turkey $1,430,000,000, Bulgaria $815,200,000. Thus the total cost for the Central Powers was approximately $60.6 billion. Costs for the Allied Powers were as follows; United States 22,625,253,00, Great Britain $35,334,012,000, France $24,265,583,000, Russia $22,293,950,000, Italy $12,413,998,000. The cost for many other nations involved on the Allied side brought the total to $125,690,477,000.[26]

What follows in this paragraph for 1912 to 1923 are the figures for the receipts and outlays of the United States government in millions of dollars; receipts are followed by outlays for each year. 1912 (693, 690); 1913 (714, 715); 1914 (725, 726); 1915 (683, 746); 1916 (761, 713); 1917 (1,101, 1,954); 1918 (3,645, 12,677); 1919 (5,130, 18,493); 1920 (6,649, 6,358); 1921 (5,571, 5,062); 1922 (4,026, 3,289); 1923 (3,853, 3,140).[27]

With the total cost of World War I to America being about
$22.6 billion, could the capitalist class have paid for the whole
conflict itself without subjecting the underclass – which, of course,
bore almost the entire cost of the war in terms of loss of life, serious
injury, physical absence from home for years, and so on – to picking
up much of the financial burden for the conflict as well? The answer
to that is an obvious yes. Today the capitalist class, the ruling elite,
have about 90 percent of all income, wealth, assets, and so on,
concentrated into the hands of just 10 percent of the population.
That was true as well in the period of World War I. A news account
published in October 1917 estimated that the United States had an
estimated wealth of $230 billion, compared to Great Britain's $86
billion, France's $62 billion, and Germany's $76 billion. At the start
of the war in 1914, the United States' debt was $1,027,000,000, a
little more than one-half of one percent of the nation's wealth. By
1917 US debt has increased to $7 billion (3.05 percent of wealth).
For that year, the estimated debt for Great Britain was $24 billion,
France $20 billion, and Germany $26 billion. As a percentage of
wealth, the debt ratio for those three was, respectively (27.90
percent, 32.25 percent, and 32.20 percent). The estimated income
of America in 1917 was $40 billion, $12.5 billion in Great Britain,
$6 billion in France, and $11 billion in Germany. The percentage
of Great Britain's debt to income was 192 percent, France's 334.34
percent, and Germany's 236.27 percent. In the United States, for
that year, 1917, the figure was 17.50 percent. Thus, America's ability
to pay was 11 times greater than that of Great Britain, 20 times
greater than France, and 14 times greater than that of Germany.
From these figures, the argument was made that Americans could
buy lots more Liberty bonds; that the country had not begun to
sacrifice. However, a more interesting figure was the cost to America
of $22.6 billion in total for the war. The nation's wealth was
estimated at $230 billion, with 90 percent of that ($207 billion) held

by the ruling elite. A one-time tax of just 11 percent on that $207 billion would have produced $22.77 billion, more than enough to meet the full cost of America's involvement in World War I.[28]

An article on the *Forbes* magazine website in 2017 by Chase Peterson-Withorn drew readers' attention to a list that appeared in the magazine in 1918 and ranked the 30 wealthiest people in America. That ranking put John D. Rockefeller at the top with (all figures in 1918 dollars) an estimated $1.2 billion. Henry Ford sat at number eight with an estimated wealth of $100 million, and J. P. Morgan Jr. was ranked in the number 13 spot, with a few others worth $70 million. Those 30 people had a combined wealth of $3.680 billion. In 2017 dollars, Peterson-Withorn put the figure at about $63 billion. However, he acknowledged that different ways existed to compute the figure in current dollars, one of which placed Rockefeller in 2017 dollars at $340 billion.[29]

But it could have been paid for by the ruling elite in a much easier way without even touching any of the non-liquid assets. On June 30, 1919, it was reported that the total deposits of the state savings and private banks and loan and trust companies in the United States was $21,744,000,000. Using the same ratio of 90 percent meant that the ruling class held about $19,569,600,000 of that amount. The capitalists' "petty cash drawer" contained almost enough money to finance the conflict entirely.[30]

Today conscription is generally accepted by the ruling classes as necessary to wage wars, at least for wars of the past that required large numbers of bodies, cannon fodder. There has never been any real debate in the ruling circles about its need. But then the children of the elite rarely ever go, even with supposedly "fair and even-handed" conscription rules. Yet the idea of conscripting the capital of the parasite class to fight wars – it was, after all, that class that initiated all wars, and it was that class that reaped an enormous financial benefit from those wars – was never discussed. It was not considered and dismissed for one reason or another; it was just not discussed, which illustrated that in a "democracy with free speech," some things cannot be and will not be discussed.

Chapter 2. Selling the Bonds.

The sales pressure on the public was relentless and remorseless during all of the Liberty Loan drives. One could not turn around or read any newspaper for more than a few pages without coming across one or more ads. The media was unanimous in hyping the bonds and doing their part or more than their part to see that the ordinary American, of low or moderate income, would be persuaded and cajoled into paying more than their share of the cost of the war that had been started by the capitalist class and which enriched the capitalist class. It was the underclass that supplied all the cannon fodder on the battlefields and thus that class already paid for the war, in terms of death, blood and injury. To add insult to injury the capitalist class also insisted that the underclass finance much of war as well.

At the tail end of the First Liberty Loan drive a Philadelphia newspaper (that city's share of the total quota was $250 million) was worried the city would not reach its goal. Thus when the Philadelphia Liberty Loan committee met one morning it issued an order to; "Go after the slackers" It was issued to the "army of bond salesmen" before they began the last lap to reach the target of $250 million. With just 11 days left in the campaign the city of Philadelphia had subscriptions to bonds that totaled just $110 million. The salesmen reportedly knew who the slackers were and would "bombard them with literature and personal visits until they enter the campaign." Also active would be the "Liberty Bond Clubs in the commercial houses and industrial plants and, it was remarked; "Appreciating that the 'little fellows,' as the small investors are styled, must enter the campaign in large numbers in order to make the Liberty Loan a success, unusual preparations have been made by the general committee to stimulate and develop the organizations." For example, the employees of Gimbel Brothers department store were to hold a mass meeting with Lewis H. Parsons, chairman of Philadelphia's Liberty Loan Committee who would make the main address and urge the clubs to get behind the campaign. A similar meeting was to be held at the Lit Brothers department store [Lit was a lower-priced alternative in Philadelphia to stores such as Gimbel Brothers]. Lit had already mailed out to its customers some 50,000 subscriptions blanks for Liberty bonds.[1]

To enlist the aid of Philadelphia trade unionists, ex-Senator Richard V. Farley, Patrick Conway and Dr. George Muller visited the Stetson plant in Philadelphia, one noon hour. A trade union sponsored automobile was scheduled to make daily trips to industrial plants during the remaining days of that First Liberty Loan drive. Theaters in the area were also involved. Many of them allowed Liberty bond orators to address their audiences and a majority had inserted the "Buy a Bond" appeal into their film programs. For example, that very afternoon Judge Eugene C. Bonniwell addressed the audience in Keith's Theatre and Judge Joseph P. Rogers spoke there that evening. It was the intention of the Philadelphia Liberty Loan Committee to raise $50 million in that city through the efforts of its 20,000 unpaid agents, of which 4,000 were Boy Scouts, 10,000 were school children, and 6,000 were "trained" bond salesmen, heads of industrial plants, business committees and women. As an adjunct to the work of the salesmen a great public demonstration was staged in the form of a Liberty bond parade, as a part of the draft-day program. A parade of 10,000 was to assemble, of which 4,000 were Boy Scouts. Reportedly that parade of 10,000 would be "representing every class of official and business life." The parade list indicated that the first division contained military personnel such as marines and sailors; the second division contained the city mayor, various Liberty Loan committee members, the police band, bond salesmen in lines of six with banners and flags, Home Defense Committee members, and businessmens' associations with bands; the third division contained "state fencibles" [an old military organization raised in Philadelphia in 1813 as part of the Pennsylvania militia]; the fourth and final division of the parade held 4,000 Boy Scouts. Note that this representative parade contained no unionists, no women, and no low or moderate income folks.[2]

An editorial about Philadelphia's last minute push to reach its quota said that after June 15, 1917, [formal end date for the First Liberty Loan issue] "the bond slacker will have lost the opportunity to redeem himself. Instant action will admit him into the patriot class. No true American can afford to miss this chance to register his loyalty."[3]

As an approximation, one could tell something was not in the best interests of the average American when Wall Street – through its New York Stock Exchange – was enthusiastically, avidly in favor of the Liberty Loan program. The New York Stock Exchange took out a one-quarter page ad in New York City newspapers in June 1917 that urged its readers to subscribe to the bond program; it specifically mentioned that installment payments were an option. As well, Wall Street pointed out it was doing this good work without charge and profit.[4]

During that same month the Liberty Loan Committee in El Paso Texas went after the slackers among that city's businessmen in their campaign. Reportedly, some businessmen had refused to invest in the bonds "so special committees were appointed to call on them Saturday and insist that they buy them." Spokesman for the committee F. P. Jones declared they would keep after the slacker "until they purchased bonds." He added; "It is the intention of our committee to hound them until they come through."[5]

Still in June 1917 a "patriotic" meeting, about the bonds, was held at the city hall in Chickasha Oklahoma. According to a journalist; "The man who pastes the American flag on the windshield of his automobile and wears a flag on his coat but who has not put his hand in his pocket to buy a Liberty bond was derided in no uncertain terms by speakers..." today. And, that reporter added; "The man who is worth from $10,000 to $40,000 who has publicly stated on the streets of Chickasha that he is going to leave it to the poor people to buy bonds was openly hooted and calls to put him on the slacker list rang through the hall." That meeting was called to order by Thomas H. Dwyer. Those in attendance were mostly all businessmen and it was claimed that the banks had done all they could "safely" do in the matter. And that it would be "dangerous" to drain the resources of the banks and leave an insufficient sum to finance the commerce of the country. In other words, it should be the lower income classes that not only fight the war on the battlefields but that they should also do the bulk of the financing. Alger Melton suggested the appointment of committees to "work the town," to increase bond sales. It was finally decided to appoint a committee of 30 men to make the canvas of the city in groups of three. An editor with a Chickasha newspaper added that; "Confidentially, we wouldn't mind seeing the kaiser send a Zepp [Zeppelin, a rigid airship pioneered in Germany by Count Ferdinand von Zeppelin] over to drop a few bombs on the blond slackers."[6]

At the end of the First Liberty Loan drive New York announced the appeal had been a huge success in its area. In an article that contained much self-congratulations it was also recorded that; "It is only the people of the cities and larger towns that have rallied to support the Government. The farmers have failed. The wheat growers of the West, the corn growers of the Mississippi Valley and the cotton planters of the South are the Liberty Loan slackers." Not only was it possible to buy bonds on the installment plan but it was also possible to buy them through payroll deductions – both of those were relatively new methods of financing in the era of World

War I. In New York City employees purchased $2.8 million worth of bonds; 35,000 employees subscribed with 26,000 of them paying through payroll deductions. On average each of those employees subscribed for $80 worth of bonds – the smallest bond that could be purchased was $50.[7]

In the summer of 1917, between the First and Second Liberty Loan campaigns a report appeared that showed subscriptions under the partial payment [installment] plan played an important part in the success of the First issue, which had a goal of $2 billion. Reports from almost 1,000 large firms and corporations showed that more than 500,000 employees bought bonds on the installment plan, 47 percent of them subscribing through their employers. According to investigator John Muir, thousands of large employers throughout the nation did not make any effort to interest employees in the Liberty Loan because of the shortness of the campaign. Bethlehem Steel's results indicated that 65,861 employees out of a total of 69,874 subscribed to the program on the installment plan at work, a rate greater than 94 percent. The total amount subscribed at that plant was $5,777,650. Muir thought that if similar "intensive" methods, such as used at Bethlehem were used by other corporations, then similar results would be obtained. With respect to the interest rates paid by the First issue of bonds the report noted; "the consensus of opinion among the small savings bank people seems to be that a rate of interest allowed on government bonds higher or as high as the average rate of interest allowed on savings bank deposits would result in great disturbance in the investment markets and result also in that disturbance in general financial conditions which we are all anxious to avoid." Admitted was the inclination on the part of workers to purchase the lowest denomination of bonds on offer, that is, a $50 bond. Muir also investigated the "attitude of labor" toward the "proposition of subscribing part of wages and salaries for bonds to be kept in the custody of employers during the period put forward. It was thought by a number of students of labor conditions that the unions and the union spirit might oppose the reposing of funds in the care of the employer." However, according to Muir, of the 1,000 corporations monitored, not one of them "reported any feeling of distrust on the part of employees such as had been anticipated in some quarters." Note should be taken of the fact that with respect to this "attitude" of labor no labor unions or trade unionists were contacted: only corporations were queried on their workers' attitudes. At Crucible Steel Company, 6,495 of 14,000 employees subscribed for bonds. At the Edison Electric Company 604 of 2,300 employees availed themselves of the $1 deposit plan to purchase the securities. At the Philadelphia Electric Company 2,100 of 3,500 employees purchased bonds. Concluded Muir: "There was practically no disinclination shown to participate on the partial payment basis because of labor union or other prejudice against such a method of saving."[8]

In October 1917 a newspaper from Vermont reported that the Second Liberty Loan drive started off with "considerable enthusiasm and impetus in the large financial centers of the country..." especially New York City. There was an official limit of four weeks for that campaign with a total of $3 billion as the target amount of money to be raised. Noted the report; "Every city, town and hamlet should have its campaigning committee, whose duty it should be to visit personally every person who is financially able to purchase one or more of these bonds. No one should be overlooked. The government needs the hearty assistance of all of us."[9]

At the start of the Second Liberty Loan drive the city of Detroit made preparations for its campaign. On a Thursday night the 10 team captains of group A, who would canvass the large manufacturing plants of Detroit, held their organizational meeting and dinner. A. A. Templeton, president of the Detroit Board of Commerce was chairman of that committee with Horace B. Peabody as vice chairman. Boy Scouts and high school cadets had volunteered to place posters in store windows and other conspicuous places around town. Posters were also to be placed on billboards in Detroit. The executive committee of the campaign had received notice from F. R. Fenton, Detroit chairman of the Federal Reserve district, that Detroit's quota for the bond drive had been reduced from $50 million to $42,742,000. The Reverend Joseph A. Vance, pastor of the First Presbyterian Church "flayed the bond slackers in a rousing talk" in addressing 100 team captains in that organization meeting. A general meeting of bond salesmen, about 1,000, was held a couple of nights later, also in the Detroit Board of Commerce building. Upwards of 13,000 school pupils were to take an active part in the campaign, as salesmen. That same week the four-minute Men held their organizational meeting. And finally, the Michigan Bankers' Association held a meeting with respect to their part in the bond selling drive. Note that the bond drive was all driven from the top down. All involved were from the wealthier classes. There was no groundswell of support from the underclasses in favor of the bonds. There was no mention of women in the organizational efforts, nor of minorities, nor of trade unionists, nor of the working class in general.[10]

A full page advertisement urging readers to buy bonds appeared in a Williston North Dakota paper on October 11, 1917. It was paid for by four banks; First National Bank, Williston State Bank, The Bank of Williston, and Williams County State Bank. One of the headlines featured in the ad declared; "Don't be a bond slacker." That appeal to buy bonds highlighted the idea that the money raised from bond sales bought food, clothing, guns, and ammunition for the soldiers in the trenches thus, with respect to the buying of bonds; "This is a Duty, a solemn, sacred Duty, which MUST be performed...The world must be purged, purified and made free." People could purchase the securities at any bank, which would take your subscription "without fee or charge for services..." That bank would also hold the bonds for the purchaser after they were issued, if desired. For those who were short of money but long on patriotism a purchase could be made with "only a Dollar Down on each bond, if you wish." In those cases the bank, or whoever put up the money, held the bond until it was completely paid for, no choice was involved.[11]

At the same time, early in the Second Liberty Loan campaign a concentrated effort was launched among the employees of the Pennsylvania Railroad. It began with an address by President Samuel Rea that was delivered to a meeting of about 200 officers of the company. Approximately 65 committee were to be organized to cover all portions of the railroad and altogether upward of 1,000 men would, in the coming days, be enlisted in the work of personal solicitation. It was part of the plan to make a personal and individual appeal to each of the 160,000 employees of the line.[12]

Also at the start of the Second drive, Washington D.C. planned a major event to kick off the campaign. It was a big day of music and oratory in the nation's capital with people who attended the event able to listen to the John Philip Sousa band and to hear United States Secretary of the Navy Josephus Daniels speak at a mass meeting. Total subscriptions to the Second Liberty Loan issue, to that point, by officials and employees of the War Department totaled $185,800 from 7,271 people – a per capita rate of $25.55. Reportedly, soldiers, officers and candidates for commission at the Fort Myer training camp also subscribed in large numbers. Mrs. James H. Boggs, president of the Woman's Wilson Union [women for US President Woodrow Wilson] appealed to all members of that organization not only to purchase bonds themselves but to try to sell to a friend or acquaintance a bond a day for 10 days. Speaking before women of the Treasury Department and the Department of the Interior Mrs. William Gibbs McAdoo [wife of the Treasury Secretary] urged women of the government departments, who could not buy a bond, to help sell a bond. Mrs. Antoinette Funk [a noted suffragist of the era] addressed both meetings, urging her listeners to buy bonds.[13]

At the start of the Second drive in Grand Forks North Dakota the manager of the St. Hilaire Lumber Company showed up at the bond committee headquarters and turned over bond subscriptions for each and every employee of that concern. From the office boy to the superintendent every employee paid a salary by the firm had, reportedly, signed up for a bond. Managers and superintendents of industrial enterprises in Grand Forks were called into conference at the committee headquarters. In each business house in the city the manager was to estimate the amount of bonds to be purchased by his employees "and by organizing his staff, and by aiding his men to make payments the task will be greatly simplified." Grand Forks North Dakota had a bond quota of $300,000 for that Second issue. According to a news story; "Big results are anticipated and so perfect is the system that has been adopted that it is believed that not a person in the city will escape the salesmen...the merchants have extended their efforts to increase the sales among their employees."[14]

Auto magnate Henry Ford, it was reported during the Second drive, had subscribed $5 million of his personal money to buy bonds while his firm, Ford Motor Company, had signed up for the same amount. Ford was well known in America then as being anti-war. With respect to his donations Ford stated; "Although there is not a man in the world more opposed to war than myself I felt we must support our government to the limit in this war." While the $5 million was credited in many accounts, as in this one, as having come from Ford, through his firm, it was actually money not from the company but from the employees. The Ford Motor Company was underwriting the subscriptions of its employees and agreed to make up any shortfall between their employees' total subscriptions and the sum of $5 million.[15]

M. J. Shaw, charged with assaulting J. W. Nickells, an Oklahoma City Liberty Loan worker on Oct 18 1917, was released from custody the next day by United States District Attorney John Fain, after he conducted an investigation. The loan worker said that Shaw moved his right hand toward his right hip pocket after he had struck Nickells, after Nickells had tried to persuade him to buy a bond. Shaw alleged that without provocation he had been called "un-American" and a "dirty slacker" by the soliciting committee of bond salesmen. Besides Nickells, the committee was composed of G. I. Gilbert and E. Guy Owens. Shaw supposedly had witnesses to back up his story, three people plus his wife. Nickells declared he and his committee used the "usual bond selling tactics" and that at no time did they descend to the "rough mechanism" attributed to them. Shaw admitted he bought no bonds from the First issue and said his failure was due to being financially unable – a condition he said was still in effect during the official campaign for the Second issue. Shaw's story was that the committee came to his place of business "with blood in their eyes" and that they "picked on him" until he jumped into his auto to escape. Nickells jumped onto the running board of Shaw's car, said Shaw, and in order to remove him so he could move his vehicle Shaw shoved Nickells "gently away." The three man committee denied that story totally. So great was the excitement created by the affair among the bond workers and at the Chamber of Commerce offices that it was decided to abandon plans for the Kaiser-shooting-in-effigy event slated for a few nights into the future, and devote the time to "a relentless chase for 'domestic enemies.'" The Oklahoma City executive committee in charge of the campaign declared it did not wish to do anyone an injustice, said C. H. Russell, one of the executive committee members. Russell added; "We realize that there are persons in this city who are unable to buy even a $50 bond. We do not wish to humiliate them. But all who are able to buy bonds and who refuse to do so, or those who buy less than they are able to carry are to be firmly dealt with henceforth." It was Russell's duty to call on the phone all alleged bond slackers reported to him. To "root out slackerism" from Oklahoma City three special committees had been appointed to call on persons whom the first visiting committees found a "difficulty in handling."[16]

Fred Shaw was a brother of M. J. Shaw who lived in Tulsa and was described as a wealthy automobile dealer in Tulsa. He said to a reporter, regarding his brother; "I told him he would get in trouble if he didn't get right with the government." He added that he was ashamed of his brother's actions. Fred Shaw had purchased bonds from both the First and Second issue - $50,000 purchased in the First drive alone. Fred expressed a desire to send a telegram to Oklahoma City officials "asking them to give his brother the limit."[17]

A full page ad that appeared during the Second bond drive in an Iowa newspaper had no listed sponsor and was, perhaps, placed by the local Liberty Loan committee. That ad featured a section on slackers, wherein it said the financial slacker "is looked upon as an outcast..." and that if you "shirk" your responsibilities "you will lose the respect and friendship of your neighbors...The fact that you have not the ready cash is no excuse. Your credit will do as well so you must see your banker today!" More ominously the advertisement stated; "You are being watched, your friends and neighbors are asking if you have subscribed. The Marshalltown [IA] committees have your name listed and are awaiting your response."[18]

On the same day the Iowa ad appeared another large ad was published, this one in an Oklahoma City publication. It was paid for by the American National Bank. It was about buying bonds and doing so on credit. Unlike other claims made by financial institutions about no fees or charges being involved in such purchases, this ad did disclose that a fee was involved. For example, for a $1,000 bond one had only to send the bank $50 as a down payment. They charged interest on the balance – in this case $950 – at five percent per year. Said the advertisement; "Please remember that you will lose very little interest, as we only charge you 5% and the government pays you 4%" on the Liberty bond. The bank was doing this, continued the ad; "entirely from a patriotic point of view" as it could loan out its money "at much better rates if we wanted to make profit only..."[19]

From time to time there emerged, during the various bond drives, as part of the selling efforts, some of the worst "poetry" imaginable – doggerel of the highest order. This one was published originally in the *New York Times*, and was reprinted in other publications. It was titled, "Buy a Bond!"

Hey! You fellow with a roll.
Buy a bond!
Show your heart is good as gold –
Liberty depends on you.
We must down the Hunnish crow,
We each have our bit to do –
Buy a bond!
If you are too old to fight,
Buy a bond!
If you lack in weight or height,
Buy a bond!
All the battles are not won
By the men behind the guns –
Money talks! Ere setting sun
Buy a bond!
If your sons have gone to war
Buy a bond!
Others' sons have gone before –

Buy a bond!
Slackers they who will not fight
Or who draw their purse strings tight,
Do your bit and do it right –
Buy a bond!
If you smoke or if you chew
Buy a bond!
Each day skip a weed or two, to
Buy a bond!
Sacrifice should pleasure be
When the cause is 'Liberty,'
That's the way it looks to me –
Buy a bond!
Everybody! Get in line –
Buy a bond!
Come on in. The buying's fine –
Buy a bond!
Crush the Huns on land and sea,
Everybody. One-two-three –
'Rah! Rah! Rah! For Liberty.'

Buy a bond![20]

A long report on the blitz type of sales campaign underway in Oklahoma City observed that all American citizens had to make sacrifices and do their part in helping the United States to win the war. That was the message delivered by A. C. Scott, faculty member of the University of Oklahoma at one of the pep rallies held to sell bonds. "I have stood on the corner in my lifetime and heard members of the I.W.W. and other such organizations talk against the government and would not open my mouth," he said, "but things are different now and when a man raises his voice within my hearing he certainly hears from me." After hearing speakers, bands, pep rallies and so forth team captains and other unpaid volunteer workers left the Chamber of Commerce building with, reportedly, more energy and determination to sell more securities. As to sales tactics, it was said; "Every kind of influence except actual physical torture was being brought on bond slackers by the executive committee this morning. 'Hard-boiled' duty-dodgers who refused to buy when first approached or who bought less than the amount allotted them, were visited again today by a different committee. If its members returned unsuccessful another committee was assigned the job. If the third committee failed, the dodger's telephone began ringing and he heard a few patriotic sentiments expressed by his business acquaintances, banker, etc. The result of this kind of third degree was that the recalcitrant generally changed his mind."[21]

A journalist in West Virginia pointed out that there were few if any slackers in England, France, Italy or Germany; "Will you back our cause with your money as well as your work and lives." He argued that none of those European countries he mentioned were as rich as America, yet each and every one, friend or foe, had successfully floated every war loan they had issued. Readers of the piece were urged to ask themselves "Am I a Liberty Loan slacker?" as it was called "a duty" to match and overwhelm the German war chest. Concluded the journalist; "Every dollar you can spare, every dollar that you save is needed by your country. Every such dollar that is not invested in Liberty Bonds is a slacker dollar and its retention in your pocket stamps you as a dollar slacker."[22]

One of the selling techniques utilized in Tulsa Oklahoma involved retail sales. The sales clerks of the Scott-Halliburton-Abbot store proved they were government bond salespeople as well as dry goods sellers on one day in October 1917 when they sold $900 worth of Liberty bonds to store patrons during the morning alone.[23]

An ad was placed in a newspaper in Bennington Vermont by the New England Telephone and Telegraph Company a day before

"Liberty Day," which took place on Wednesday October 24, 1917, as a special day to work intensively on selling bonds. Many businesses were expected to shut down that day and civil servants were given the day off work, all to push bond sales. New England Telephone and Telegraph announced in its ad that its office in Bennington would be open but devoted solely to the sale of Liberty bonds on that day.[24]

On the same day in the same newspaper a large ad addressed to "Mr. Citizen" appeared. It was paid for by "a local merchant" and raised the issue; "Do you realize it is just as dishonorable to be a Liberty Loan slacker as it is to be a military slacker?" The bulk of the text of the advertisement told of the enormous sacrifices soldiers had made buying bonds. They were paid just $30 a month but it was said that for a whole fort the soldiers therein had subscribed, on average, for five $50 bonds each. That meant they agreed to have a payroll deduction of $25 each month [from the $30] for 10 months. Reportedly even the soldiers in the guard house, for minor infractions of the rules, subscribed "to a man," all 38 of them. It was Fort Ethan Allen in Vermont.[25]

One of the strategies employed in Philadelphia to pressure people into purchasing the bonds was the erection of "safety gates" on the street, guarded by a "corps of young society women." The gates were similar to those used at level crossings for railroads and were meant to indicate to passersby that it was dangerous to pass without subscribing to the Liberty Loan campaign.[26]

Worry about lagging sales caused some officials to look for someone to blame. At the end of October 1917 the federal government had, reportedly, started an inquiry into the activity of pro-German and pacifist "propaganda" conducted in those districts of Illinois that failed to support the Second Liberty Loan drive. Joseph B. Fleming, Assistant District Attorney was in charge of the investigation. No county in Illinois fell below 90 percent of its allotment but, it was said, several counties were financially able to subscribe far more than they did "and the apathy is ascribed to the activity of pro-German and peace propagandists." Attention was also drawn to the fact that those same districts were laggards in the first liberty loan." It was an odd argument especially considering that the mainstream press was completely in favor of the bond programs and never had a single word to say against them, even in the form of mild criticism. As well, organized labor was uniformly in favor of the program. The few groups that may have opposed the bond sales had no access to spread any "propaganda" save perhaps handing out material on street corners.[27]

A similarly intense effort was made to sell the War Savings Stamps. When famed preacher of the day Billy Sunday made an entrance into the Washington D. C. War Savings Stamps drive in January 1918 it added impetus to the campaign of the D. C. committee. At a "patriotic rally" to sell the stamps Sunday asserted; "You are a darn good for nothing mutt if you haven't bought any war savings stamps yet." Two prominent women came to Washington to assist in that drive. One was Mrs. Rupert Hughes, wife of the novelist; the other was Mrs. Coker S. Clarkson. An aim of the central committee of fraternal orders in that city was; "Every lodge member in the District a war saver."[28]

A large ad that appeared in a Washington newspaper for War Savings Stamps, when Sunday was in town preaching, addressed the "unpardonable sin" of extravagance. To buy an article at that time was to take away from the government the time, the labor and the material that went into making it. It was time for people to shake off extravagance and buy War Savings Stamps. That message to do away with needless buying came from United States President Woodrow Wilson.[29]

The War Savings Stamps program also was the cause of its own share of doggerel poetry. The following was sourced out to a newspaper in Illinois, the *De Land Tribune*. It was titled "Just you."

If you are too old to fight,
Buy a Stamp!
If you lack in weight or height,
Buy a Stamp!
All the battles are not won
By the men behind the guns –
Money talks; ere set of sun
Buy a stamp!
If your sons have gone to war
Buy a stamp!
Other sons have gone before –
Buy a stamp!
Slackers they, who will not fight,
Or who draw their purse string tight;
Do your bit and do it right –
Buy a stamp!
If you smoke or if you chew,
Buy a stamp!
Each day skip a weed or two, to
Buy a stamp!
Sacrifice should a pleasure be
When the cause is 'Liberty'
That's the way it looks to me –
Buy a stamp!
Everybody! Get in line –
Buy a stamp!
Come on in, the buying's fine –
Buy a stamp!
Crush the Huns on land and sea

Everybody! One, two, three –

'Rah! Rah! Rah! For Liberty!'

Buy a stamp!

It bears a striking resemblance to the earlier poem about buying Liberty bonds.[30]

An ad that appeared for the War Savings Stamps program in an Oklahoma newspaper bore the headline "Will you save a soldier's life?" That was a recurring theme in advertisements for both the Liberty bond drives and the War Savings Stamps campaigns. That is, the idea that soldiers in the battlefields would somehow go without food, clothing, weapons, and so forth, if those at home did not buy the securities and thus prevent the soldiers in the field from being starving, naked and defenseless.[31]

Credit men were reportedly at work and uncovering Liberty bond slackers among business houses in whose financial surpluses were "all that could be desired from a financial point of view." Edmund Wright, described as one of the leading credit authorities of New York, said that in checking up on the financial statements of many concerns engaged in various businesses in all parts of the United States the percentage of Liberty bonds of the First and Second issues "included among their assets was startlingly small." Other credit men were said to have observed the same condition and it had been suggested that banking institutions would be fully justified in bringing to the attention of their customers, particularly those who are borrowers, the necessity for these patriotic investments being made in "reasonable proportions." Wright declared that with the Third Liberty Loan issue about to be floated attention should be drawn to the lukewarm attitude of many business houses in upholding the government in its prosecution of the war."[32]

An article that appeared in an Ogden Utah newspaper at the start of the Third Liberty Loan campaign carried the subhead; "Every home is expected to make arrangements to buy at least one bond and banks will help by extending credit." The local committee in Ogden was reported as ready to go and just waiting for a supply of index cards that were to be used by the local committee to record the results of their visits to people as they sought to sell the securities. When the county and the city had been thoroughly combed over the list of loan slackers – those who had not subscribed and who had "no very good reason" – would be compiled and "probably" published in the newspapers. Bankers in the area had met and made plans "that will enable every person in the community to own a bond." Those bankers had decided that not more than $500 worth of bonds could be taken on the installment plan. With respect to the $50 bonds the initial payment was set at $5.75 covering one installment and interest and then payments of $7.50 each month until the bond was paid for. According to a reporter; "it is thought that there is hardly a household in the city which could not purchase a bond by exercising a little thrift and sacrificing a little."[33]

In each city the canvassing workers were broken down into a number of teams and assigned districts to cover, and expected to call on every home and business premises in their areas. Thus, no matter what the size was of the city each person could be expected to receive canvasses at the door, and repeated canvassers at the door if the first contact failed to produce a sale. For example, in Oklahoma City each team captain had a list giving the prospects to call on. That list had the figure it was first estimated the prospect ought to spend on the purchase of bonds – his allotment. That figure was followed on each person's card by the figure that was actually expended by him on bonds in the Third issue drive. A person was in trouble if the sum spent by him was less than his listed allotment. In that case his name was added to a special list "and particular missionary work will be done by the teams in his behalf." That meant he would be called on again and "a very simple argument used that the opinion of Uncle Sam, based on what Uncle Sam has learned from the prospect's friends and neighbors in the community, is that he should do more..."[34]

According to a Seattle reporter; "While countless men are giving their lives to halt the Hun, too many are holding back their fortunes." Faced with that situation volunteer workers in the Third Liberty Loan drive planned to awaken the people of Seattle to "the immediate crisis." Even more pressure was exerted on the bond salesmen after Treasury Secretary William McAdoo advanced the goal of that campaign from $3 billion to $5 billion which, said the reporter, "almost doubles the responsibility of every American." While many in Seattle had faithfully subscribed "there are too many subscribers who have taken out enough bonds to get a button but have, in reality, failed to shoulder their proportionate financial burden." In order to insure there was 100 percent compliance in the drive from the Cascade division of the Great Northern Railway, W. A. McLeod, chief clerk to the assistant superintendent of the dining room and sleeping car service had "framed the names of the 14 men in his division who have not subscribed for bonds and hung them conspicuously in a busy RR station...He expects the men thus receiving undesired publicity to step up with checks in the near future."[35]

An ad placed by the Citizens Bank, Flagstaff Arizona branch, declared there was no difference between the slacker in military service and the financial slacker. The advertisement declared that both were, in effect, "disloyal" to the government.[36]

Another article from Seattle complained that the take up of the Third Liberty Loan securities was not fast enough and, said the article; "There are too many dole slackers – income cowards."

J. W. Spangler of the Seattle National Bank was also chairman of the Chamber of Commerce war council's drive. He declared that he felt "humiliated by the faint-hearted response of Seattle business men to the government's request." Shipbuilder D. E. Skinner said; "These money slackers ought to be exposed for not responding in proportion to their incomes." Spangler also backed the idea of a "showdown." According to the journalist who produced this story; "It is probable that hundreds of able men, who fail to take subscriptions in proportion to their incomes, will be checked up. Plans for special inquiries, and possible publication of lists of the financially disloyal, are being outlined." At that point the Chamber of Commerce estimated that "practically 13 percent of Seattle's population had subscribed to the Third bond issue, which was short of the benchmark of 20 percent set by Treasury Secretary McAdoo. That 20 percent goal of having one out of every five people buy a bond extended across all of the United States. So, concluded the newsman, Seattle needed to enroll seven percent more of its population "if Seattle is to be straight-American."[37]

During the Third Liberty Loan drive it was reported that an estimated 5,000 Ogden Utah people had bought Liberty bonds but there then remained 1,855 who had not made purchases; "These will be given until the last day and if they have not subscribed they will then be 'visited' by the individual committee which will get down to a frank basis with them and get a loan or a good reason for not getting one"[38]

One of the key days during the Third issue campaign was a single day late in April 1918 designated as "Liberty Day." No less than 40,000 Liberty bond holders were expected to march in the Liberty Day Parade to be held in Washington D. C. on April 26. During the one day that remained before the parade the local bond committee devoted much of its focus on people in the area who had not purchased securities "and liberty bond slackers will be diligently sought after and proof of their subscriptions will be asked for." US President Wilson had designated Friday April 26, 1918 as "Liberty Day" and had made the afternoon of that day a holiday for all federal employees throughout the nation "for the purpose of lending to the success of the Third Liberty Loan."[39]

An advertisement that urged the reader to buy War Savings Stamps gave specific detail about what the purchase of a stamp would do in furtherance of prosecuting the war. One thrift stamp would buy a tent pole, a waist belt or shoe laces; the purchase of two stamps would buy a pair of woolen gloves. Twelve stamps purchased would buy a steel helmet. One War Savings Stamp would buy 100 cartridges, or a cartridge belt. Two and a half would buy a gas mask while the purchase of three War Savings Stamps would buy an overcoat; four would purchase a rifle.[40]

Bridgeport Connecticut became the first city in the Second Federal Reserve District (NEW York), with a population over 100,000, to meet its quota in the Third issue drive and was then close to hitting 1.5 times its quota, with a full week left in the official campaign. The Second Federal District included all of New York State, a bit of New Jersey and Fairfield County Connecticut. Despite going over its target city officials in charge of the bond drive joined forces with the city police in a last minute push to sell even more securities. The executive committee of the local group met with police officials and it was agreed to have police officers visit every home where a Liberty Loan certificate was not displayed to find out the reason why it was not and it was reported that "the police are now actively engaged in rounding up the Liberty bond slackers." There was also a push on at the factories. A "normal" push that did not involve the police. The Bullard Machine Tool Company related that every employee of the plant had purchased a Liberty bond. The 1,672 employees had subscribed for bonds totaling $107,000. An "honor flag" to show the factory's 100 percent subscription rate was raised at the plant with "simple ceremonies."[41]

During the last few days of April 1918 leaders of the local bond drive committee in Ogden Utah, chairman A. G. Fell and secretary O. J. Stillwell, had been engaged going over the list kept at their headquarters checking up to see who was supporting the issue and who was not, in Weber County. After another day it was planned to implement remedial measures to "bring the 'loan slackers' into the fold of good Americans." In all of the theaters of the city that night Four-Minute speakers were to appear and tell of the necessity of subscribing for Liberty bonds. Those speakers, said a journalist "have unselfishly given their time and ability to aid the campaign and good results have been achieved."[42]

An article that was published in a Louisiana newspaper discussed the role of the federal government with respect to its role with the local Liberty Loan Committees. According to the piece those committees were urged by the federal government to cover their territory fully and not cease their efforts to sell Liberty bonds until everyone had been approached and urged to subscribe. The federal authorities did not hesitate to say to the committee that they were "drafted" for the work and were not to stop until after the drive was over. Said federal officials to the local committees; "If anybody refuses to buy bonds who is able to do so, require that they sign a blue card giving reasons for not subscribing." Treasury Secretary McAdoo was said to be particularly anxious that everyone purchase a bond and even if a community exceeded its quota that fact "should not benefit slackers. Persons able to subscribe, but who have not done so, should not be allowed to escape doing their duty because their fellow citizens have responded generously and promptly." Advice from the federal officials continued; "Remember that you are drafted for this patriotic work and that you must keep at it until you get your honorable discharge on May 4th [official end of the Third issue drive]. There must be someone in your district who has not yet subscribed – HE IS THE MAN YOU WANT."[43]

Women were used extensively as volunteer workers to sell bonds but they were virtually all found at a low level in any and all of the various Liberty Loan Committees. As a result they were rarely mentioned. Children were also used extensively in canvassing efforts, principally the Boy Scouts. One example could be seen in the photograph that showed Agnes Brockie and Sarah Franklin buttonholing E. P. Lineaweaver, vice president of the Commercial Trust Company in front of his office in Philadelphia. The two women were Emergency Aid workers "and have figured prominently in all three Liberty Loan campaigns."[44]

That the man who gave little or nothing to the bond funds that were needed to buy America's defense was not entitled to that defense, was a point made by J. W. Hoopes, of the Federal Reserve Bank at Dallas Texas, in a communication to a reporter. He argued; "That one man shall give all and another nothing is morally indefensible." Hoopes also observed that the word "sacrifice" was used advisedly. "The man who has $400,000 and invests $5,000 in Liberty bonds has made a sacrifice, it is true, but to what extent has he sacrificed? The difference between 4.25 percent and the interest he would have earned by the investment in, let us say, his business – whatever that may be. Does this entitle him to the use of the allied fleets – the blood and tears – the sweat and agony of the armies of civilization?" Concluded Hoopes; "Unless you have given up something – denied yourself something – you have not paid your way, you are a moral defaulter – worse, far worse, than a man who refuses to pay his trade debts. Where do you stand?"[45]

One pitch to Americans to buy bonds supposedly came in the form of a soldier's appeal to the "comrades back home" to buy

Liberty bonds as the way to back the fighting man. It was made by William Dougherty of the 309th Ambulance Company, then stationed at Fort Dix New Jersey. He urged the home folks not to be slackers in coming forward as subscribers "to the full extent of their means." Said Dougherty; "The individual who refuses, or even reluctantly purchases a single baby bond [a $50 bond] knowing that he could conveniently purchase more, is as much a slacker as the man who refuses to fight for his country in these dark and threatening times."[46]

An article that appeared in a New York City newspaper in May 1918 took the form of a supposed conversation between a bank cashier called Mr. Paine and a bank customer named Jimmy Telford. In explaining why he could not buy a bond Telford told Paine that he had no cash. You do though, replied Paine, you only think you haven't any cash. Telford said he only had $25 on deposit in the bank and that he owed the grocer $40, the butcher $60, he hadn't paid his last coal bill and he was overdrawn on his salary for the next two months. Paine asked his customer when he though he could be in a position to make the first payment on a bond. Not until the summer was the reply. Telford admitted to the bank employee that he had purchased no bonds in the First issue and no bonds in the Second issue as he had no cash at those times either. Paine then confided to Telford that he was in the same position himself, as his customer. But he and his wife went out and put a chattel mortgage on all their furniture, pawned all of Mrs. Paine's jewels and then "loaded up on Liberty bonds." Telford thought that was all great and congratulated Paine. As a bank employee Paine's salary was $5,000 a year. He also argued that everyone lived too high, spending as though their salaries were larger than they really were. "We've forgotten something that we never knew – how to save money," lectured Paine. He then supposed that if the government should publish in the newspapers the name of every man who had not bought a Liberty bond "there'd be a fine scramble, wouldn't there, for bonds?" But suppose the government went further and had a sort of "excuse me" column in which it placed the names of men who were excused from buying bonds because they couldn't afford it; "Gee whiz, we'd sell our souls before we'd have our names in that column wouldn't we?" Paine also admitted that he had pulled the same stall as Telford, saying he would buy bonds next week, next week, and so forth. Telford asked Paine how he planned to get back those jewels and pay off the chattel mortgage on the furniture; "Easy, our tremendous passion to keep up appearances will take care of that. We'll starve and freeze to get back those jewels – that's second nature." Paine concluded his lecture by urging Telford to sign up, to talk it over with his wife and to put the money down at "his window" in the bank within the next 10 days. The reader was then informed that Telford did put the money down, inside of two days after receiving Paine's lecture, instead of 10 days.[47]

An appeal from federal bond authorities at the Treasure Department in Washington on May 1 1918 went out to all local Liberty Loan Committees to inaugurate an intensive finish for the Third issue drive and to see that no possible subscription was overlooked. That appeal contained 12 suggestions of things that could be done to make the Third campaign a success. One suggestion was to inaugurate a "buy another bond" campaign to get subscribers to buy more. See that employees of every industrial plant had been canvassed creating, if possible, committees of employees to complete the work. To see if all stores and offices had been canvassed. Obtain publicity to the fact that the desired 20 million subscribers meant one bond buyer to every five people, practically one bond to each family. "Many wealthy men and large institutions are holding off on account of paying large income taxes," and any people or firms should be reminded of the necessity involved in the drive. Follow up on all pledges made to ensure they were turned into actual subscriptions. Check to see if committees in areas where the quota had been reached or surpassed were aware of the "necessity of continuing the battle for large over subscriptions and wide distribution." And; "See that individuals and firms which benefit from war business increase their subscriptions in adequate proportions."[48]

With the lull that occurred in 1918 between the hype over the Third issue and the Fourth issue of Liberty bonds, publicity focused more on the Thrift stamps and the War Savings Stamps program. In New York City a streetcar had been fitted out with Thrift stamp slogans, with Uncle Sam and Miss Liberty on board as the crew. Its appearance on the streets of New York was calculated to speed up the sales of securities in that program.[49]

Another example of commercial tie-ins could be seen in an ad for Goldstein's Emporium in Juneau Alaska. That advertisement was touting women's clothing and collars but also featured small panels in the ad – two of them that urged readers to "Buy Liberty Bonds" and two that hyped War Savings Stamps.[50]

The Idaho State Council of Defense adopted a resolution in May 1918 stating; "That the county councils of defense all over this state be asked to call before them any persons in the county who have not purchased Liberty Bonds, and give them a hearing and find out why they have not bought bonds and then if, in the judgment of the council, they are able to buy bonds, have not and still refuse to, that the county councils publish their names in public places and newspapers, branding them as unpatriotic."[51]

A full page ad appeared in a Barton Vermont newspaper urging people to buy War Savings Stamps. That advertisement was paid for by several individuals or firms such as Jersey Star Creamery, D. A. Brahana, Sears and Russell, Ezra Taylor, and Irasburg Vermont. The text of the ad stated, with respect to those who could afford to purchase bonds but did not, that they were "deserters pure and simple. And, the text continued; "There may be some who can honestly say that they cannot afford an occasional quarter for a Thrift Stamp. We don't happen to know any, but we are willing to concede that some poor people can honestly offer this excuse."[52]

Early in June 1918 a committee of Chattanooga Tennessee merchants started on a canvass that was to include every merchant in the city. These merchants were to be pledged to buy and sell as many War Savings Stamps as possible. A list of the cooperating merchants would be published, as well as a separate list of those merchants who did not cooperate with the committee. "From time to time the work being done by the merchants will be published and if there are any lagging they will receive some unfavorable publicity," said a news story. That was the plan of the retail merchant's committee of which Adolph Mathis was the chairman. And, it was also noted; "For the state the plans are made so that every family who does not buy nor pledge themselves to buy war savings stamps will be reported to the state director's office. These reports will in turn be sent to Washington with the address and reasons for not buying." At that point; "This will easily determine any unpatriotic persons in the state, and although it has not been revealed just what will be done by the government it is expected that unless excellent reasons are given for not buying they will be looked up and treated as slackers." On Friday, June 28 all taxpayers and wage earners were to be called upon to meet and hand in their subscriptions for war savings stamps. Officials conducting those meetings, would keep a record of the proceedings and report the names of all persons present and the amount of War Savings Stamps subscribed for by each; "The names of absent persons and of those who refuse or neglect to subscribe, with their reasons for so doing, will also be reported."[53]

A fairly large collection of poetry urging people to buy War Savings Stamps was gathered together and published in an article in a New York City newspaper. All were eminently forgettable, as were the earlier ones hyping the Liberty bonds. One was notable in that it was written by Ring W. Lardner;

There was a foolish man,
And he bought a foolish block
Of Yaki Hula Common.
A foolish mining stock.
And now he dines on field mice,
And pals with other tramps,
Which never would have happened

If he'd bought War Savings Stamps.[54]

With the start of the Fourth Liberty Loan drive to begin it was announced that the quota for Oregon was to be $45 to $50 million to be raised. In comparison Oregon's quota for the Third issue had been $17.5 million – in the end $27.5 million was raised. Robert E. Smith, Oregon state manager of Liberty Loan campaigns said, because of the dramatically increased quota; "it would go hard for liberty loan slackers in October." Smith added; "The big feature of the next campaign will be the comprehensive and unfaltering way that so-called 'slackers' will be handled...the campaign is to be organized so thoroughly that when a man refuses or fails to buy his quota, not only will he be asked to give reasons, but his reasons will go on record."[55]

When the Northern California conference of Liberty Loan chairmen held a meeting in San Francisco in late August of 1918, after the Third issue and before the Fourth issue, one of the big questions discussed was what was to be done with slackers. Although "strong arm" methods were discouraged full "moral suasion" was endorsed as a tactic and it was the opinion of Governor of the Federal Reserve Bank 12th District, James K. Lynch, and a majority of chairmen that names of those refusing to subscribe, after being given a hearing, should be published in the newspapers as a "Badge of Shame." Reports were made by chairmen that members of certain religious sects and pro-Germans of several stripes were "stubbornly refusing to buy bonds." It was agreed, among the participants with respect to methods that "diplomacy obtained the best results."[56]

In advance of the Fourth Liberty Loan drive officials in Idaho announced that a check was to be made on the bond slacker during that campaign and, stated a news account; "those found delinquent may be required to wear what will be termed a 'badge of shame.'" Information to that effect reached the committee in charge of the Idaho State campaign, from the 12th Federal Reserve District headquarters in San Francisco.[57]

At the start of September 1918 there was a brief article about an order promulgated by the Public Safety Commission of Minnesota. By the terms of that order "all persons refusing" to purchase their allotment of bonds may be required to give testimony regarding their financial condition.[58]

At a meeting held by the Morrison County Minnesota Liberty Loan Committee, with R. B. Millard as county chairman, it was the unanimous opinion at that meeting that the allotment system was the only fair one to use in determining the value of bonds each person should purchase. Each precinct within the county was to select a committee of from three to seven men, or more, to allot each man; "the amount of bonds that is only right and fair that he should take. If he refuses to buy bonds and is well able to do so he will be classed as a loan slacker and a sworn statement as to his financial condition will be taken and sent in to the state headquarters to be put on record."[59]

Related to the poetry that sometimes appeared in conjunction with the bond sales were the shorter and more succinct slogans. Some of those included:

Wear your old clothes and buy Liberty Bonds.
Liberty Bonds or German bondage.
'Come across' or the Kaiser will.
The soldier gives; you must lend.
Liberty Bonds or German taxes.
Buy over here to win over there.
It's billions for defense or billions for indemnity.
A bond slacker is the Kaiser's backer.
A man who won't lend is the Kaiser's friend.
The more bonds you buy the fewer boys will die.
Be one of the million to lend the billions.
"Dig up the coin and bury the Hun.
Idle dollars are pro-German.
Put the 'pay' into patriotism.
Bonds speak louder than words.
If you can't fight, your money can.

Freemen buy bonds; slaves wear them.[60]

Cashing in bonds or War Savings Stamps was almost as great a sin as not buying them in the first place. A report from Indiana noted that War Savings Stamps "slackers" continued to show up at the post office in Richmond Indiana with their excuses for cashing their stamps. One explained that he wanted to cash $3,000 worth of War Savings Stamps so he could buy larger amounts of Liberty bonds (on the installment plan) and thus make a "better showing." Post Master Beck said there was a general rush that week to cash the stamps and more money would have to be paid out than was expected to come in. Said Beck; "Robbing Peter to pay Paul" doesn't win the war.[61]

The Fourth Liberty Loan Train Number 1, carrying carloads of trophies fresh from the battlefields of France, 12 speakers and a Naval band of 25 pieces, began a trip of 4,198 miles through California, Arizona and Nevada on September 23 1918. The train

would stop for two hours or more at nearly 150 cities during its
itinerary which ended at its starting point, the Oakland California
pier on October 19, after 27 days on the road. One official on board
was John A. Britton, chairman of the general publicity committee of
the Liberty Loan for the 12th Federal Reserve district.[62]

Late in September of 1918 F. S. Viele, chairman of the Liberty
Loan Committee for Yavapai County Arizona outlined his plans for
raising the county's quota for the Fourth issue drive. In the Third
campaign the county had a population of about 18,000 and secured
6,600 subscriptions – a rate of about 34 percent. He suggested that
if a man wished to buy a $500 bond he should split it up and put
the smaller bonds in the names of family members. For example, a
$50 bond for each of his two children, a $100 bond in his wife's
name and a $300 bond in his own name. That way the county would
have the names of four people on its subscription list, instead of just
one. Viele remarked that there were 125 owners of automobiles in
Prescott who had not subscribed to the bonds and; "I suggest that
a careful canvass of all automobile owners be made to the end that
every man who drives a pleasure car should be the owner of at least
one Liberty Bond." It was also reported that many mining companies
and other concerns in Arizona were accepting their employees
subscriptions taking from 10 to 25 percent down and allowing the
payments to be made in monthly installments so as to complete
the payments in six to eight months. The banks were willing to do
the same. With respect to slackers Viele suggested that a list of all
who refused to subscribe be compiled along with the reasons for
not subscribing. Also suggested by him was the formation in each
community of a committee whose business it would be to go to those
who refused to see if their refusal was justified. Said Viele; "We leave
it to the judgment of the committee in each community to decide
what action shall be taken in case of a person who is able to subscribe
and who refuses. But we advance as a theory that cannot be gainsaid

that anybody who is not with us in this thing is against us, and anyone who is against us is not entitled to share in the benefits of our government or the advantages that each community secures from the existence of the government."[63]

Whatcom County Washington appointed its own Liberty Loan Slacker Committee just before the start of the Fourth issue drive, at the request of the chairmen of the various districts and vigorous methods "will be taken to round up those who can afford to buy bonds but refuse to do so." The committee planned to consider all cases reported to it from all sections of the county. Those accused of being slackers would be invited to appear before it and would be given a "fair hearing" before any action was taken. "A plan that was approved at the county meeting and which could be adopted would be the publication of a "Slackers' List, in which are enrolled those who fail to square themselves with the Slackers' Board."[64]

At the same time it was reported that the United States Treasury Department had asked Lynden Washington to purchase $75,000 worth of Liberty bonds in the Fourth issue drive. That quota was double Lynden's target for the Third issue drive, of $37,500. In that earlier drive Lynden over subscribed reaching a total of $59,000 in bond sales. A rule-of-thumb basis with which committees all over Washington state would work with "is a month's wages in bonds from every wage earner..." So important was the need for this backing of the war effort, it was said; "that the committees are authorized to recognize but two things that are more important than the purchase of bonds – food and clothing. Food, clothing, and Liberty Bonds next, is the order in which the needs should be met." With respect to individual allotments, it was reported; "Each individual will be requested to appear before the board, and consult with it as to the amount of his subscription...a effort will be made to allot each individual with a fair portion of the total bonds. Injustices worked by this preliminary estimate will be adjusted by the Board."[65]

Also at the end of September it was noted that a large amount of work was being done then to prepare the vigilance committee of the El Paso Texas Liberty Loan drive for its work. A card index system of all subscriptions to the First, Second and Third Liberty Loan drives as well as a system of record of every business and residence in El Paso was being prepared for use of the vigilance committee allowing them to reach "all those who have heretofore not subscribed, also those who have not subscribed according to their means...All loyal citizens are expected to report bond slackers to this committee..."[66]

That El Paso Texas vigilance committee announced it was "going after the Liberty bond slacker with a vim and vigor that will stir them to coming out of the shameful position they have taken in regard to purchasing bonds." R. M. Dudley of the vigilance committee added; "All prominent men, heads of corporations large and small, whose taxable property is greater in proportion than the amount they have subscribed will have their names published in the newspapers and the amount subscribed, and their names will also be read before the vigilance committee at one of the future luncheons. This applies to all business, no matter how large or small they are." An example cited by Dudley was the owner of a drug store who had been assessed as being able to purchase $10,000 in bonds but had only bought $100 worth.[67]

Worried that Grand Forks North Dakota would not achieve its quota for the Fourth issue drive the executive committee of the local Liberty Loan campaign declared; "It is hard to imagine that there are any Liberty Loan slackers in Grand Forks, yet this seems to be the case. We have made appeal after appeal, but the response has been lukewarm. The people still are lethargic; something must be done to stir them to a deep realization of their duty."[68]

A warning against selling your Liberty bond came from the editor of a Hawaii newspaper early in the Fourth Liberty Loan campaign. Said the newsman; "You do not help the government...when you buy a bond during the flush of enthusiasm which comes over you during the bond campaign only to sell it later." He urged his readers to; "Buy you bonds and then lock them up. Put them out of temptation's way. Forget them when it comes to figuring them as an immediate asset." Whenever a person sold his bond the new purchaser, therefore, did not buy a new bond. Also, he argued, selling a bond could depreciate the price of those securities in the bond marketplace. And that hampered new sales.[69]

An article from a California newspaper contained the melodramatic subhead; "Blood on your hands if you do not purchase bond, says speaker." According to the reporter who covered that speech; "Right down into the heart of the Liberty Loan slacker, Galen Lee Rose drove his shaft; right into the bilge of the bond evader, the disloyalist, the pussyfooter he drove his spearheads of truth, when he spoke to a large audience..." Rose also thundered; "If you do not buy a bond the blood of these crusaders [US soldiers] is upon your hands. Dare you break faith with such as these?"[70]

In Philadelphia there were also worries about reaching their quota for the Fourth issue drive. With one-third of the campaign time over the area had reached only one-tenth of its goal. The influenza epidemic – which went on to reach historical proportions in America – was said to be a major factor in the slowdown. But, nevertheless, remedial steps were implemented; "Employers throughout the entire district have been asked by the industrial section solicitors to purchase bonds for their employees, relying upon the workers' patriotism later to take over the subscriptions. This method of boosting the sale of the new bonds would reach all workers, including those confined to their homes after having fallen ill with influenza." This method, of course, meant purchasing bonds for their workers without any formal authority being granted and thus obligating those employees to pay for those bonds, again, with no authority being granted. Later that month in Philadelphia members of the local Liberty Loan campaign and the four-minute men would "co-operate with the employers who follow this plan to show employees why they should take over the bonds held 'in trust' for them by their employers." A derogatory name for some slackers was "button buyers." It referred to people who paid a few dollars down in the previous three campaigns, received buttons showing they had subscribed and then they promptly forgot about the obligation they had incurred and paid no more on the bonds purchased. Wearing a bond button on one's clothing was considered "proof" of purchase, patriotism, and so on. More importantly, it afforded protection against being harassed on the street by bond solicitors and, during these drives, those salespeople tended to be everywhere all the time. Street harassment was a common problem, and only the wearing of a button as "proof" would forestall it. For the Fourth Liberty Loan drive the per capital quota for the Philadelphia district was $75; the per capital quota for the city of Philadelphia itself was $144.[71]

Two small ads appeared on the same page of an Arizona newspaper on October 7, 1918. One urged readers to wear their Fourth Liberty Loan button, to show you were an "American," while the second one was about not being a "contemptible" bond slacker, on whom words should not be wasted.[72]

Phoenix was another city that worried, during the Fourth issue drive, about being behind in reaching its quota. As a result it launched a crackdown on slackers; "The type of person who imagines he can 'get by' with the purchase of a fifty-dollar bond, or a subscription of $100 when he is perfectly capable financially of multiplying those amounts by ten or twenty, will not be exempted just because he had made a subscription. Nor will the fellows who invariably inform solicitors that they have already subscribed, and then refuse to give the amount or the name of the bank, be allowed to go unchallenged." Also not to escape was; "The man who tries to sneak by with the assertion that he always subscribes through his bank and then does not come across, and the fellow who puts off the soliciting committee with the excuse that he wants to subscribe through somebody else, will all be given no rest until they have bought bonds and satisfied workers at headquarters, who by the way have an exact record of every purchase of bonds in previous loans, that they have bought to the full measure of their ability."[73]

One week later Phoenix stepped up the pressure when the local officials in the bond drive announced the formation of a "shock committee" consisting of seven "prominent" citizens. The group was to be in session at the Liberty Loan headquarters for the remainder of the campaign for the purpose of investigating cases of persons who had not subscribed in proportion to the "amounts that should be rightly expected from them." It was stated that many who could buy more were trying to get by with a single $50 or $100 bond. The shock committee was to be assisted in its work by the "reconsideration committee." That group would first call upon those who, in its judgment, were not buying enough. If the reconsideration committee met with opposition or if the person approached failed to show "good and sufficient" reasons why his subscription could not be increased the case was referred to the shock committee. If all that failed the names of such persons would be given to the public. The committee declared it; "will appreciate receiving from the public the names of any persons whose subscriptions should be investigated. All cases reported will be fully investigated, and in no instance will any person's position, wealth or standing in the community result in their exemption."[74]

The race to achieve its quota was also beset with problems in Philadelphia and that slowness toward the target led to a drive against the Fourth Liberty Loan slackers in the district. It was noted that, with respect to slackers; "there are many." The Saturday in that week was designated "Conscience Day," which was meant to be the culmination of a three-day blitz against slackers to be held to boost bond sales. All those listed as slackers in the area were to be visited during that blitz period when a special effort was to be made for them to "do their bit." Aided by the various draft boards of the city, loan workers were attempting to determine who had not done their share. For example, in one section of Philadelphia "in which there are few houses of the class in which poor people live," the Liberty Loan investigations had learned that out of 138 men who registered in the previous month for selective service, there were only five who held bonds of any of the four issues. All of those men who had not bought bonds were married; there wives were healthy and no children were dependent upon them. All were employees and their incomes ranged from $1,200 a year to $12,000 per year.[75]

When Raleigh North Carolina was also faced with a slow pace in its efforts to attain its Fourth issue quota an article came out in favor of what was called the Des Moines plan, which could be explained as "diplomacy, denunciation, deportation." That is, said the article; "The first committee solicits, the second turns on the light; the third rides the slacker out on a rail."[76]

Another ominous article that was designed to pressure the slacker into purchasing securities appeared in a Mississippi paper in the middle of the Fourth issue drive. A subhead of the piece warned that the; "Stigma will remain upon the slacker long after the war is over." Also pointed out was that; "One by one the men who have refused and are refusing to buy Liberty Bonds are being found out." According to this piece slackers had an easier time in the First and Second drives because it was taken for granted that all who could buy a bond would do so; "People did not look as closely for the button on the coat and for the Liberty Loan flag in the window as they are looking now. The man who walks the streets now without some visible sign and emblem that he is a bond purchaser is followed by eyes that grow angry as they watch him. The house in any neighborhood that is without a bond flag in the window is a marked house. People stare at it curiously. They eye it resentfully." It will last, that resentment, long after the war is over, thought the journalist; "He will be pointed out as long as he lives The memory of his failure and his weakness will be held against his children." And, in conclusion; "the man who does not buy is finding it harder than ever to hide his shortcomings. He is being found out and in the vast majority of cases the proper punishment is being applied by those around him."[77]

An ad placed by the Olympia National Bank in Olympia Washington was titled, "Smoke out bond slackers!" In listing the various types of slackers to be smoked out, several of the six categories mentioned those who were wealthy and made fortunes out of war work but had not purchased securities in proportion to their financial condition. Questions posed by the ad to its readers included; "Do you know your action in this Liberty Bond sale is a matter of public record – open to the gaze of your neighbors and business associates, and to the nation?" "Are you willing to let the entry opposite your name stand as it is?" "Would you like to see it in the public press?"[78]

An open letter signed by J. H. Brown, Grenada County Mississippi chairman of the Fourth Liberty Loan drive in that area pointed out that Grenada County was behind in its quota and urged his audience to purchase more bonds. He blamed the shortfall on the slacker; those who had bought no bonds at all and those who failed to subscribe according to their means. Brown argued that if Grenada failed to meet its quota the "blight and disgrace" would fall on all the people in Grenada, not just the slackers. "This being true, the bond slackers who make their paltry dollars at the expense of the blood of their fellow citizens and live among patriotic, public-spirited and high-minded people, should be made to pack up their belongings and move away to more congenial surroundings – preferably to Germany itself. The list of slackers should be made public that all people might know who is for us and who is against us," thundered Brown. "Those wretches who are able to buy bonds and who absolutely refuse because they think they can make more money in other investments, should receive the scorn and indignation that will result from the righteous wrath of an aroused public opinion."[79]

Another article about lagging sales in the Fourth issue drive purported to show that big business was getting behind the effort to reach the target of raising $6 billion in nation-wide sales. Said banker J. P. Morgan; "Corporations in large numbers are holding meetings to reconsider and add to their subscriptions. Individuals are arranging to borrow who have never done so before. We urge every subscriber to double his former subscription and to turn it in at the earliest possible moment." A massive rally was held on Saturday October 19, 1918, to mark the official close of the Fourth campaign. According to a journalist; "Important bankers are urging that buyers of the Fourth Liberty Loan wear their buttons to-morrow [Saturday the 19th] so that the bond slackers may be picked out."[80]

In that last day or two of the Fourth campaign a Seattle newspaper wrote about the "official mouthpiece of Washington – it has 40,000 tongues. It is known as the Division of Four-Minute Men." That is, there were a reported 40,000 speakers on file as part of the Four Minute Men, all of whom stood ready to deliver short, patriotic messages on a variety of topics, in various settings, from street corners to theaters. The branch in Seattle had 55 men "with strong voices and 100 per cent patriotism certificates." In King County there were 150 such men. All 40,000 worked through the Committee of Public Information, headquartered in Washington D. C., under the leadership of George Creel. Their duty was to talk for four minutes on any subject that Washington recommended, as often as directed and at as many places as directed to. Their subjects were all sent out by the bureau in Washington but the orators "write their own speeches." Topics they pontificated on included Americanism, mobilizing manpower, Liberty bonds, and War Savings Stamps.[81]

At the very end of 1918 a campaign was launched by the War Savings Stamps officials. One aspect of that campaign was the issuance of new posters that were displayed all over America. The posters bore the title; "Are you a W. S. S. pledge slacker?" That campaign was in response to an investigation made by the War Savings Stamps authorities of the pledge cards that had been signed by people who pledged themselves to buy so many stamps during the drive of June 1918. That drive ended on December 31 and in order to meet the quota, all pledges made in June had to be redeemed. A little over 60 percent of those who pledged had either bought none at all, or only a few of the number pledged. However, many of those who made pledges purchased more than they pledged to acquire. The pledges were made direct to the United States Treasury.[82]

By then the war was officially over and all the hype about selling Liberty bonds and War Savings Stamps and Thrift stamps came to a sudden stop. Also coming to a halt was the frantic and virtually unanimous attacks on all those defined as financial slackers. There were some attacks on those deemed shirkers during the Fifth Liberty Loan campaign that began in April 1919 and was officially the Victory Loan campaign. However, the enthusiasm and almost religious zealotry that attached itself to the persecution of slackers during the four Liberty bond issues, especially the Third and Fourth, was lacking. After all, the war had, by then, been over for five months. But some held grudges, and had longer memories. Speaking to the Baltimore chapter of the American Institution of Banking in May 1920 was M. M. Prentis, manager of the Baltimore branch of the

Federal Reserve Bank. In that speech he flayed those Liberty bond slackers and declared that Liberty bond purchasers who had sold their bonds at below par, since the war ended, were "four flushers" and indirectly responsible for the present high cost of living.[83]

Chapter 3. Editorials, Opinions, Attitudes, and Threats.

Opinion makers of the era offered many thoughts on financial slackers. Leading the way were editorial writers with newspapers. Still, others, such as religious figures and politicians, were not absent from the discussion. All opposed the financial slacker; nobody bothered to mention that the failure to buy bonds or contribute to the Red Cross or YMCA in their war work did not violate any law. Yet the condemnation was universal and often vehement. Extreme rage and thinly veiled threats often made their way into the commentary of society's "best and brightest." When violence was inflicted on the slackers, as it often was, it perhaps found its roots, motivation, and rationale in the rantings and ravings that often came from the "opinion makers."

One of the earliest to voice an opinion was banker John W. Staley, a vice president of the Peoples State Bank of Detroit and the executive manager of the Liberty Loan campaign in the Detroit area. According to Staley, the bank's customers had subscribed $2.5 million during the First Liberty Loan drive. He offered the thought that those who could subscribe and did not subscribe to the bond drive were in a class with the slacker who was planning on dodging his duty to his country by not registering for conscription. At the same meeting, Staley gave his opinion was Abner W. Larned, who also scored slackers. At that meeting of the Liberty Loan sales committee, Larned declared slackers seemed to think that subscribing for bonds was a sort of charity. Said Larned, "This is a defense measure. We are not going to ask anyone's charity." As well he criticized the manufacturers, not because they did not subscribe, but because they did not come down hard enough on their employees to ensure they bought bonds; "I am sure that there is not an employer in the city who could not organize his factory and put his share of the loan over in a half-a-day..." if he had put effort into the endeavor.[1]

"There must be an army at home behind the army at the front...investment in the Liberty Loan which is, in itself, an expression of confidence n the United States of America," thundered an editor with an Indiana newspaper. However, he did admit that the "low rate of interest may not be attractive." respond in the negative – or maintain a shamed silence – to the interrogation, 'Have you bought your Liberty Bond?'...It is either a Liberty Bond or the shackles of militarism...Don't be a bond slacker."[2]

Opinion makers were just as livid whether the slacker refused to buy Liberty bonds, War Savings Stamps, or to donate to the Red Cross. "You may be too old to go to war or there may be other reasons why you would be exempt from armed service, but there is no age limit to enlistment in the Red Cross and there are none who are exempt for any other reason, except that they are too poor to join. The Red Cross needs you now. But there is no conscription in the Red Cross. You must volunteer. If you don't you are a Red Cross slacker," explained a Pennsylvania newspaper editor. He added, "Slacker isn't a pretty name. But if you don't join now or during the progress of the campaign that is to be started next Monday when you look in the mirror thereafter you will behold the face of a slacker...You will see, in that event, the reflection of one who thinks more of a dollar bill than he does of his country – for the Red Cross is a branch of the national service in war-time, and a membership may be had for as little as a dollar. Surely there are none such in Harrisburg."[3]

During this period, Billy Sunday was very famous and perhaps the best-known of the religious figures then in vogue. During his sermons in New York City in June 1917, many thousands turned out to hear him speak. According to a reporter, "Billy stopped long enough in his preaching in the afternoon to explode somewhere around a million pounds of verbal high explosives under slackers, anti-conscriptionists...and a few others of his pets." Said Sunday, "We haven't much use for the slacker who didn't register, and I want to tell you that we haven't much use for the slacker who won't buy bonds and help finance the war. And slacker and traitor are both spelled with the same number of letters. I want to see every man here wearing a Liberty loan button."[4]

About four months later, Billy Sunday addressed a meeting in San Francisco on behalf of the Second Liberty Loan campaign. "Make your dollars hit the trail," he enthused. "Kick in with the coin and kick out the kaiser," he told the thousands of people who gathered to hear the famous preacher roast the Liberty Loan slackers and the German emperor in the same sentence.[5]

Indiana was reported to be covered with Red Cross flags in July 1917, urging all to do their share in raising the $1.5 million as the state of Indiana's proportion of the $100 million wanted from the nation for the beginning of its campaign drive, called herein a "philanthropic endeavor." The editor of an Indiana paper declared, "Ignorance of the campaign and its purpose will not avail any 'slacker' who seeks to evade his fair share of this donation to the country's cause." And, he continued, "From national headquarters comes the command – the Red Cross must stand behind the man behind the gun. When you are solicited this week by a Red Cross lieutenant, don't turn him down." Before the editor launched into a long tirade about the urgent need to give, he observed, "We have raised a Y.M.C.A. fund; we have subscribed our part of the Liberty Loan; we have furnished money for many an enterprise which has keenly urged itself upon us."[6]

According to one report, "Nothing was said at the time, but Morrow County [Oregon] had a few slackers in the Red Cross campaign. They were slackers of the worst sort too, for it is well known how these men have gained their wealth from a land of free and...liberty loving people...It seems that the HOG spirit sometimes takes possession of a man's soul until there is not soul left at all; if there is, it is the soul of greed," thundered an editor with an Oregon newspaper. He continued by stating, "It is very likely that every man of known wealth who had an opportunity to aid the Red Cross and did not, will be advertised far and wide and may the day come when the government which has been so good to him, will use a force sufficient to bring him to his knees in repentance. His worldly wealth is dearer to him than all honor. He stands a good chance of losing both."[7]

An editor from a Newberry South Carolina publication remarked, "We take pleasure in commending Gov. [Richard Irvine] Manning [SC] for his manliness in retracting his statement that every man who was able and did not buy a liberty bond was a 'slacker' and a 'traitor.' He is quoted as saying, 'I did not intend to call these men traitors.'" Said the editor; "Simply because a man does not whoop and hurrah is no reason to call him a traitor or a slacker. Those are harsh words."[8]

"But what about the financial slacker?" mused the editor of an Oklahoma newspaper. His wondering was rhetorical only, as he had the answer. "Well, he is the worst of all...he is to be despised. While it might be too rabid to suggest that he be driven out of town, that's the sentiment of real patriots." However, he did note that the wealthy could lend their money out, or invest it and "they can make their money earn 6 percent!" So, he wondered, why buy a four percent bond. For that query, he had no answer.[9]

An editorial writer with a West Virginia newspaper gave much effusive praise to the Liberty Loan program, its need, and the idea that it was the anchor of security. "The present is more favorable for the taking up of this issue of the Liberty Loan than when the first issue was exploited, when a billion in excess of the requirements was obtained. The season's crops are practically assured, a year of unusual prosperity in nearly all sections of the county will be soon completed...What is holding people back, then? The sacrifices we are called on to make are pitiful enough when we think of what our soldiers are doing and what they will be required to do."[10]

An editorial from a Montana paper pointed out that in the first year of the war, Germany floated loans totaling $3,386,000,000, or about $48 for each of its 67,616,000 people. The United States government was then asking for a new loan of $3 billion (Second Liberty Loan), which would make a total loan of $5 billion in the first year of the war. As America had 101,577,000 people, it amounted to about $40 for each person. Germany was then in the 4th year of the war and had just put over its 5th loan. All that information caused the editor to speculate that patriotism in the United States must be at a very low ebb since Americans subscribed less than Germany in its first year of the war. Then the editor urged his readers; "Let us not be slackers but make the record of Missoula county so good that the people of other counties will be envious of us."[11]

Writing in Richmond Virginia, in October 1917, a newsman tried to shame the home folks. He wrote that the response from American soldiers to the Liberty Loan campaign was, while a "splendid tribute to their patriotism," at the same time "a reproach to bond slackers among our civil population, whose dearest interests they have offered their lives to protect." The editor continued, asserting, "There is scarcely a bond slacker in any of the military encampments in the country. Of the total issue, the indications point to the soldiers taking a large portion of it. The smallest wage-earner in the county is equally well able to subscribe for a bond as the best paid enlisted soldier" Newly enlisted soldiers were paid $30 a month.[12]

An editorial in a Seattle, Washington newspaper on the topic appeared in a box in the middle of page one instead of in its usual place on the editorial page. "Surely a man's blood cannot be red if, at a time like this, he does not loan to his country every dollar he can spare," bellowed the editor. "For remember this, you cannot alibi to your own conscience. Be a one-hundred-per-cent American and hold your held high!"[13]

"Since the beginning of the world war the term 'slacker' has taken on a special use and meaning. Today it is only applied to those individuals who shirk their duty to their country in its great struggle," an editor from Oregon informed his readers. "In England it was mainly used in connection with those men who refused to fight for their country, but in the United States it carries its greatest degree of odium when applied to those individuals who not only remain at home, enjoying all the comforts and blessings of their government, but refuse to give of their earnings, made possible by the men who have offered their lives for their safety and protection." And, he emphasized; "there cannot be any excuse whatever for a man who selfishly shirks his duty and refuses to buy at least one Liberty Bond...If the people won't loan the funds voluntarily, the government may be forced to take it...No matter what your condition, don't be a slacker."[14]

George Ade was one of the famous people of the time who came out against slackers. Ade was a well-known newspaperman, reporter, and playwright. He produced a newspaper column that was a fable about the man who sat around doing nothing, not helping and so forth, when the ship was burning down because he knew lots of other people would jump up to save the ship from sinking and thus, he could get away without helping. Concluded Ade, "Don't perch on the fence when you see your neighbor's house is burning. Don't sit on a coil of rope when the ship is sinking."[15]

An editor from South Carolina hyping the soon-to-start officially, Liberty Loan number three noted that some people aided the war effort by becoming soldiers while others were at home in America building munitions. And that; "Still others are only called upon for financial and moral backing. We are all soldiers together. A slacker is one who does not do what he is able to do. The man who can and does not buy a Liberty bond is a slacker."[16]

For an editor writing for a Colorado newspaper, the issue came down to the fact that the man who could buy bonds and did not "is a slacker, and a sight meaner citizen than the deluded alien who unwittingly lets fall a word of his ingrained adoration for the Kaiser. Yet we demand the Dutchman be locked up or killed, while the miserly slacker who refuses to bear a share in financing his government – he's a pretty good sort of a fellow you know, only a little 'close.'"[17]

One religious figure of the era, the Reverend Elmer T. Clark, a Methodist minister from St. Louis and a former secretary of the St. Louis Ministerial Alliance, went so far as to prepare a prayer for the Third Liberty Loan drive for use by clergy on Liberty Loan Sunday, April 7, 1918. The campaign began officially on April 6. That prayer read, in part, "In this time of crisis and judgment, inspire us to think, act and serve together in the common cause of a victorious righteousness. Touch our souls with a high sense of patriotic sacrifice. Consecrate our means as well as our men. Bless, we beseech Thee, the Third Liberty Loan with the benediction of Thy benignant favor. May no act or word from us impede its sanctified will. And arouse our enthusiasm to see it through to a most successful conclusion."[18]

An article from Philadelphia was mostly about sales in that city lagging somewhat and with city officials hoping for an improvement.

Labor leaders in Philadelphia were said to rapidly bring their men into the drives with rallies at industrial plants throughout the district. Union leaders also met to pledge no strikes of labor men during the war. Edward Keenan, president of the Central Labor Union in that city, declared Liberty Loan slackers were not worthy of belonging to a union during that national crisis. Said Keenan; "If a man is so strong in his sympathy with the Central Powers [Germany, etc.] and is a Liberty Loan slacker, I say throw him out of the union."[19]

Senator Reed Smoot of Utah declared, "If the bonds are not subscribed, the Government will have to resort to the less favorable method of securing the needed funds by its power of taxation...The head of every family in America should purchase Liberty Bonds. Every child should be the possessor of war savings certificates." And he added, "Shun the slacker and treat every traitor as a traitor."[20]

One of the famed actors of the time was William S. Hart, described as one of the "enthusiastic advocates" of the Liberty Loan program. Said Hart; "He should at once, and cheerfully, give a little of his goods that his country has secured for him [when asked to financially contribute]...When my country asks me for life or for money I cheerfully offer both."[21]

When United States President Woodrow Wilson opened the Third Liberty Loan drive in Baltimore in April 1918, he stated, "The loan we are met to discuss is one of the least parts of what we are called upon to give and to do, though it itself is imperative. The people of the whole country are alive to the necessity of it, and are ready to lend to the utmost, even where it involves a sharp skimping and daily sacrifice to lend out of meager earnings." And those people, Wilson stressed, "will look with reprobation and contempt upon those who can and will not, upon those who demand a higher rate of interest, upon those who think of it as a mere commercial transaction."[22]

Another well-known person to speak on the issue was author Roland G. Usher. He wrote a gushingly patriotic piece that went on at length about patriotism, duty, and so forth. He asked who wouldn't feel ashamed if they had kept their son out of the ranks of the military if the son wished to go. Usher continued, "You know perfectly well that you would probably feel ashamed before your neighbors if they know that the boy was sticking at home. But have you ever asked yourself whether you felt ashamed that you were keeping your dollars tight in your jeans instead of lending your dollars to the war as well as your boy? If you have not got a boy you probably would feel that he ought to go if you had one. You have got some dollars why don't you send them?" He added, "But I will wager anything you like that you have a lot of money that you can lend to the government without hurting yourself at all, and which you are hanging on to until it screams." Speaking about a hypothetical neighbor's boy who was serving in the war, Usher emphasized that; "your failure to lend your money to the government is going to result very probably in depriving that particular boy of things he needs," at the front to wage war – such as food, ammunition, proper clothing, and so on.[23]

Actor Charlie Chaplin was another celebrity of the day who worked on behalf of bond sales. On April 19, 1918, he spent a few hours in Sumter, South Carolina, not as a "laugh-provoking clown," but as a "serious and patriotic worker for the Third Liberty Loan." In Sumter, he gave an "earnest and forcible talk" on the Liberty Loan and urged everyone to buy "bonds and more bonds." Reportedly, much money was raised that day in bond sales, thanks to the Chaplin appearance. It brought Sumter County over its quota. According to a journalist, "but the campaign will not be called off and an active canvass will be waged to obtain additional subscriptions. Every loyal citizen will be given an opportunity to buy a Liberty Bond and every slacker and secret enemy of America, who is able to lend money to the country that affords him a home and a means of livelihood will be made to show his colors. This Liberty Loan campaign is to be a show down and a show up. Those who are not for us are against us. Keep up the campaign until every loyal man or woman who is able to buy a bond has bought one and until every slacker and enemy who will not help win the war has been exposed. The time for soft talk and devious methods to keep from hurting some slackers' feelings has passed."[24]

An editor cited New Zealand, which was raising a war loan and considering enacting a law that any man able to buy a bond but who didn't could be arrested and fined double the amount of his income tax." Lamented the American editor, "In this country there is no such law, and the only punishment legitimately incurred by the bond slacker is the contempt of his fellow-citizens. Where it is openly bestowed it has been effective as a means of selling bonds to men who would gladly have evaded their duty to buy them."[25]

Financial slackers among men of great means who refused voluntarily to support the United States government and the war by placing a fair share of their wealth in Liberty bonds should feel the pressure of federal law; US Representative Julius Kahn asserted in an address to members of the Green Room Club in New York City, "The American people generally – especially the men and women of moderate means and the poor – are doing splendidly in support of the Liberty Loans," said Kahn, "but there are others of immense fortunes who are doing nothing to aid the Government or to carry on the war. It is the man who has great wealth and is not giving it, or a decent part of it, that I want to get after." Concluded Kahn, "If he does not give up I want a law enacted to compel him to do so" because there are those of wealth "who are doing practically nothing. Those are the men who will be called to account by the

Government – the man who can but won't – and the Government will get them."[26]

When Oklahoma City reached its quota of bond sales for the Second Liberty Loan drive, an editor for one of the community's newspapers urged the city to go on to oversubscribe; "A few rich men in this town still hold back. Strong arm committees are calling on them this week. It is humiliating to consider that some prosperous men in this city don't come forward with their funds at a time like this, but remain in hiding until dragged forth from under the bed and made to subscribe to a fund which every real patriot participates in without being asked." The newsman thundered the time had passed for having any patience with financial slackers, "They are not desirable citizens. They had prospered amazingly here in Oklahoma City, not so much through their own efforts, but by reason of the fact that town builders went right along and created here a great municipality. The financial slackers, tight wads then as now, quietly grew rich from the fruits of the work of their fellow citizens." He argued the city had been "rather patient" with them, "those financial slackers, who have profited at their neighbors' expense, who have become opulent through the diligence and the aggressiveness and the city loyalty of men who made the town grow, and our patience is slipping. The rich slacker has no place now in this loyal community. HE MUST BE MADE TO GIVE! We are ready now to over-subscribe our share of the bonds. The time has passed for pleading with the financial slacker. The time has arrived when he must be FORCED to realize where his duty lies."[27]

An editor with a New Mexico newspaper declared the financial slacker to be worse than a soldier slacker because; "Comparatively speaking, our financial slackers appear to be almost wholly in one class – if class may be so distinguished – and that is the so-called middle class – a class neither wealthy nor poor." And, he added, "The other two classes – the extremely wealthy and the poorer class, confined to wage earners, appear to be meeting the situation without a murmur." This journalist was puzzled and found it difficult to conceive of an "American who thinks more of a dollar than he does of his government and the principles for which it stands. Yet the bond solicitors daily encounter this class. It is about time for the government to conscript dollars as well as men." He concluded, "The financial slacker is worse than the soldier slacker. The latter gives while the former merely loans. The soldier is asked to give all; the man who buys bonds is only asked to loan a part."[28]

In a lengthy editorial in a North Dakota paper, the editor looked at some of the articles that dealt with the issue of the slacker. One of those pieces spoke of the types of bond slackers. One was the "pro-German at heart" who used "the mean treason of passive resistance – doing all the harm he can without taking any risk." A second type of bond slacker was the "willful dead beats who deliberately choose to sponge on their neighbors by taking all the advantages the United States offers and shirking as many obligations as the law permits. The third type were those not in category one or two and who "are merely lazy and lukewarm, their philosophy is 'Let George do it!'" However, it all came to the same thing in the end; indifference and selfishness came to the same end, as did those who operated as serviceable allies of the Kaiser. Frank E. Wade, chairman of the Liberty Loan campaign for Martin County Minnesota, and Clifford E. Jones, Public Safety Director, announced that all residents of the county who failed to purchase bonds would be asked to appear before the executive board of the County Safety Commission and explain why they had not bought bonds. Eighteen subpoenas for alleged loan slackers had been placed in the hands of the sheriff. Fifty more subpoenas were to be issued, it was announced. One citizen reportedly subscribed to $300 worth of bonds after the sheriff subpoenaed him. Said Wade; "Martin County proved its patriotism by exceeding the Liberty Loan quota by more than $325,000 in one day, but there is no reason for letting slackers get away."[29]

That North Dakota editor wrote two long paragraphs on duty and then launched into a section on war financing. "The fact is that the borrowing of money for the war is a necessary government activity in which the people must cooperate. The money must be raised. It will be raised. It is discretionary with the government whether the required funds be received as a loan or collected as taxes. In actual practice both methods are used. Taxes are levied up to the amount which it is believed wise to collect in that manner, and the rest is demanded as a loan. The individual is not asked what taxes he would like to pay. The tax is levied according to a fixed rule, and then the tax is collected. If it is not paid, the property of the individual will be seized and sold. No credit will be given, and no excuses will avail." He argued that the amount an individual would subscribe to the loan was left to his judgment – within reasonable limits. "This is done in order that the public may be inconvenienced as little as possible. But it is not done in order to permit individuals to shirk their obligations. The obligation of every individual to subscribe to each government loan to the extent of his ability is just as great and just as binding as his obligation to pay the taxes that are levied against him. And, while the methods of enforcing that obligation against would-be shirkers may be a little different from those employed for the collection of taxes, it is being made very clear that they will be made effective, and that the individual who tries to shirk his bond obligation is likely to find himself in as undesirable a position as the man who tried to dodge the payment of his taxes."[30]

A telegram from the New Orleans Cotton Exchange received by the United States Treasury Secretary William McAdoo (who was the federal official in charge of the bond program) purported to give as an excuse for the poor showing of the South in subscribing to the Third Liberty Loan, the fear of price-fixing of cotton provided for in a pending piece of federal legislation. However, an editor declared that the bill had received no legislative consideration since its introduction and was destined to get no consideration in the future; "That ought to be assurance enough for the South to render the excuse of the New Orleans Cotton Exchange ridiculous."[31]

After he congratulated the people of Tonopah, Nevada, who subscribed to Liberty bonds, the editor of a local newspaper then wondered about those who did not subscribe; "Some of them were easily excusable, through weakness of themselves or those dependent on them, or for other good and sufficient reasons." What about the others? "Ignorance kept some of them from subscribing, while others did not do so because they do not subscribe to the principles upon which America is founded, because they are not willing to do anything for the land where they gain their sustenance. If it were not for the shortage of labor at present in the United States, some of these slackers would receive notification to move on. The Liberty bond slacker is, in plain language, an undesirable necessity."[32]

Treasury Secretary McAdoo was described by one editor as having his heart in the right place when he called all who sold their Liberty bonds slackers. Said the journalist, "It is true that no American should sell his Liberty bonds if he can possibly avoid doing so. He should think twice and dig deep into his resources before adopting this last resort." However, the editor noted cases of necessity where an American was perfectly justified in turning over his bond and needed to feel no guilt in doing so. For example, in his "patriotic enthusiasm," a person may have oversubscribed and overextended himself. "The risk of this slacker talk is that in future loans Americans will hold back and not subscribe to their limit for fear of incurring somebody's cause if they should fail of their hopes and be compelled to sell out. The situation calls for sense

and clear statement, not indiscriminate name calling, he suggested,"
concluded the editor.[33]

Worrying that sales were lagging during the Fourth Liberty Loan drive caused an editor of a New York paper to assert, "That is bond slacking, an offense against good citizenship...who should excuse who can take Liberty bonds and do not do so?" And, he continued, "No man who has a bank account is safe from a demand that he shall take bonds according to his deposits. No man who owns a foot of land is safe from a demand that he should take the bonds apportioned to him according to his property. No man who pays rent is safe from a demand that he shall take bonds according to the resources of which the payment of rent affords presumptive proof. No man who has made an income tax return is safe from a demand proportional to the ability thus revealed." Concluded the editor; "Even more certain is it that either by the loan, or in other ways less agreeable, all that our soldiers overseas want must and will be provided. The Federal Government is speaking softly now, but it carries a big stick."[34]

Within a few weeks of the official end of World War I, another editor with a New York City newspaper urged his readers to keep buying bonds even though articles in the media were starting to appear saying the war was over or almost over. This writer tried to instill guilt. With respect to the slackers, he wrote, "Each individual among them, each man and woman of their sorry company, must carry to his grave and beyond the grave for all eternity the knowledge that so far as lay within his power, he or she did the utmost to bring triumph to the cause of barbarism and to betray the men who offer their lives for us...But the punishment will come to those who fail in their duty, as surely as patriotism and enlightened self-interest will make the Fourth Liberty Loan a success."[35]

A war exhibit train passed through Alma, Michigan, in October 1918 and drew a big crowd. Dixon C. Williams (a wealthy manufacturer) of Chicago represented the speakers' bureau of the Liberty Loan organization in Washington. He gave the primary address to the crowd that had come out to see the war exhibit. A reporter describing that speech stated it was "a hot one from start to finish and which must have gone deep under the hides of slackers" and that people at the gathering heard "the loan slackers given one of the worst combings over that they have ever received in this section of the state."[36]

Then there were the extreme editorials and opinions from the editorial writers. An Oklahoma City journalist declared there was no trouble getting patriotic people to subscribe to Liberty bonds. Still, there was a lot of trouble in getting "unpatriotic men" to respond. He felt their dollars should be drafted. "Yet we have no way right now of drafting the money of those who seem unwilling to perform their part of the duty in this crisis. It is proposed to post the names of the financial slackers so that real patriots will be able to see who are obstructing the movement that is to bring peace and security for the world," stated the editor, who then got extreme in his attitude. "Merely posting the names of these financial holdbacks, who cling to their money with the grip of a miser, is a milder treatment than they deserve. We must find a way to draft their dollars, legally of course; in times like these a mere blacklist is not a punishment that fits the crime."[37]

Furious at the idea people were not buying enough bonds during the Second Liberty Loan drive, an editor with the *New York Times* fumed; "While the soldiers are sacrificing their futures and preparing to risk their lives, the county is doing half what it ought if it is to keep its contract to clothe, feed and arm the defenders of democracy. It sounds like a betrayal of trust." Then the editor added an ominous threat; "The American who holds no Liberty bonds, either now or when this war is over, ought to be a marked man, under suspicion either of his sanity or his loyalty. Inability to take a bond is not an excuse, unless it is proved, and the burden of proof ought to be on the man or women who ought to take the bond, and not on those who ask that the bond shall be taken."[38]

A two-panel editorial cartoon showed a character named Everett True listening to a friend explain why he didn't buy a Liberty bond. True responded to the man's excuses by punching him out. Other True editorial cartoons in the slacker series appeared in the same newspaper during a week in the middle of October 1917. That was during the Second Liberty Loan drive. They all featured True with a person who had not bought a bond. All the cartoons ended with True using physical violence on the slacker.[39]

A letter to the editor appeared in a Philadelphia newspaper from "a Patriotic American." He lamented that halfway through the Second Liberty Loan drive, only 20 percent of the target amount of $3 billion had been raised. He felt there was no logic involved in such behavior as people were not asked to give money to the government but only to lend the money, and at a "good interest" He concluded that; "These people should be branded not as slackers but as traitors." More than a little illogically, he stated that soldiers – paid $30 a month – were buying $50 and $100 bonds.[40]

With respect to native-born Americans who could have helped the Liberty Loan program but did not, an editor of a Washington state newspaper declared, "They are not good citizens. If they do not like the government and do not think it is worth defending, they ought to leave this country. If they like the country, want to remain, and think it ought to be defended against a foreign foe, but want some one else to pay and do the fighting they should be deprived of citizenship. They ought to be branded, as Cain was branded." Concerning the immigrants in America, the journalist stated that when those men refused to buy liberty bonds, "they become guilty of the grossest ingratitude. Indeed, it is not certain their naturalization papers can not be removed; under the law as it now stands, an effort will be made, we are told, to pass a law by which the property they accumulated under the false pretense of loyalty can be confiscated in the name of the government and all such sent back to the country from which they came."[41]

A furious editor with an Idaho newspaper began his tirade by stating, "Don't patronize any business man, no matter what his line if you know he is disloyal...Make it your business to know whether the people with whom you do business are for or against the government; for or against the Red Cross, for or against the Liberty Loan; for or opposed to the Y.M.C.A. in its Army and Navy work. When you know a man is disloyal don't patronize him. If necessary send your work out of town to a man or firm that is loyal. In the name of Clearwater county boys who are now gone to make the supreme sacrifice for us at home, see that no unworthy wretch who would stab our men in the back is fed on your business."[42]

A final check by the Liberty Loan committee of Stark County, North Dakota, at the end of the Second Liberty Loan campaign, noted an editor, "discloses the fact that there are a few men in this town [Dickinson] who did not buy bonds though they are perfectly able to do so." And, "We cannot conceive why any man, even the salaried fellow, cannot afford..." to buy. This newsman believed there were just two reasons that could be advanced by a person for a failure to purchase bonds. One was that the man's income might be so small as to preclude his sparing $1 a week, and the other was that "he is not in sympathy with the Government. It was, he felt, unreasonable that the first cause should be advanced by anyone in Dickinson because a Liberty bond was negotiable and could be turned into collateral the day after purchase, "therefore the stern hand of the law should hover over those who are derelict. If there are any undesirables in

Dickinson, a change of residence would be acceptable...The slacker is the Kaiser's relief committee"[43]

Frank A. Kennedy was a minor political figure in Omaha, Nebraska, and a member of the district appeal board with the local Liberty Loan committee. In a speech he gave before the Concord Club in Omaha, he said that every man who has either been exempted from the military draft or given a deferred classification and had not purchased any bonds or War Savings Stamps, provided he was able, should be forced into the trenches.[44]

"No coaxing or pleading should be vouchsafed a Liberty Loan slacker. He was a slacker to begin with, if he refused to purchase Liberty bonds when financially able to do so in accordance with his rating," grumbled an editor in Oregon. "The mere fact that he would 'come through' with persuasion, does not make him a patriot nor lesson skepticism as to his loyalty. Mental status should of course be taken into consideration, before judging him too harshly, but where there is an absence of affiliation with the Red Cross or the Y.M.C.A. endeavors, it would be hard to condone even that."[45]

Holding similar views was an editor from Arizona; "Purchasers of Liberty Bonds may be slackers. The possession of one or more bonds does not entitle the holder to exoneration from the stigma of being a slacker. Only when a person has purchased Liberty Bonds to his full ability, can it be said that he is not a slacker." He went on to add that slackers had been found in the Warren district of Bisbee, Arizona – that was a wealthy section of the city. "They are of the under-purchasing variety, of the clique and caste which buys one-tenth of what it should buy in order to stand on the curb and boast of possession of Liberty Bonds...They refuse to assist the district, and thereby aid the nation to their fullest ability, when they are called on to lend to their government." Discovery of bond slackers in the Warren district was made when it was announced that the Honor Roll of bond purchasers would be published. "Committees canvassing the districts began to receive requests not to make public the subscriptions they received. The banks were overwhelmed with similar requests...Why should not a resident of this district wish his name published in the Honor Roll? Why should he wish to retain secret his subscription to the Third Liberty issue? Why should he request his pledge to their greatest of causes be suppressed?" Since the federal government has requested that every name and pledge amount to the Third Liberty issue be published in community Honor Rolls, the editor argued there was only one answer to the questions he had posed; "The man who would keep secret the sum he has subscribed is a self-convicted Liberty Bond slacker. He knows deep down in his own heart that he has not pledged to the government as much as he can afford. He is conscious that he is shifting the burden to others. And he knows that if his subscription is published others will know he is a slacker. In the face of these facts, he takes advantage of 'banking courtesy' to request that he be protected from a public whose right it is to know." According to the story, the officers in charge of that campaign in the Warren district had announced that they would publish the details of all subscriptions that came into their hands. "They have declared themselves in favor of recognizing the government's request," declared the editor. "Among their duties is the discovery of slackers in this drive. They do not believe that any purchasers of Liberty bonds is due the 'courtesy' of suppression. Rather, they believe each individual shall buy to the limit, and be proud to have a place in the Honor Roll. And, they are looking with suspicion on those who have requested that their names not be published."[46]

"If you own as much as $1,000 worth of taxable property Uncle Sam has your name and counts you as one able to buy a Liberty Bond of at the least a $50 denomination...It is known by the government that 3,000 persons in Maury County [TN] are able to buy Liberty

Bonds, but at noon yesterday only 587 persons had made application for bonds," explained an editor with a Tennessee paper. He thought only about half of those who could buy bonds were on that list of 3,000 and that no one knew what to do with those slackers. He noted that various methods of dealing with the bond slackers had been suggested and adopted throughout the United States. Still, from a Mississippi city came a report that it had adopted a "most appropriate" treatment for the slackers." That city planned to publish a list of names of all those "who failed to respond when the government called, who was willing to let the boys in uniform risk their lives for Liberty while he held with a miser's clutch to his dollars and failed to buy for Liberty..." Furthermore "the patriots in this Mississippi town are going to ostracize these slackers. The man whose name appears on that list is going to find himself in an uncomfortable position as the 'man without a country.' He is going to find the back of every hand turned against him. He is going to realize that he lives in a city of patriots where the possession of a few dollars will not buy respectability." The editor concluded that although such a drastic method as that used in the unnamed Mississippi town might not be adopted in other cities, including his own; "the attitude of the public toward Liberty Bond slackers should be the same everywhere. The truth will be known and the patriots of Maury are going to uphold the honor of the county."[47]

Reaching lofty heights of hyperbole, a North Carolina editor fumed, "And the man who is able to buy bonds and yet persistently refuses to do so is the most contemptible creature on the face of the earth. He is a far worse slacker and coward than the soldier who whines and deserts. The deserter has at least the excuse of physical fear and desire to save his worthless hide; but the bond slacker has not the soul of a louse; he betrays his country for a few dollars and has not the shred of decency that would have him go out and hang himself."[48]

Equally outraged was an editor with a Colorado publication. "The man or woman residing in America, who refuses to buy Liberty bonds at this critical time, be he or she whatever nationality, deserves nothing better than comradeship with the mongrel rule of the Central empires. They should sit at the table with the kaiser and bask in the sulfurous fumes of his hateful presence." He added that no Montrose Colorado "patriot wants anything in common with blond slackers. We shouldn't even share the sidewalk with them. They ought to be pushed off in the ditch and made to walk there. Strong, eh? Well not half as strong as the stench to the nostrils of a patriot that a bond slacker makes."[49]

Comparing the bond slacker to "the coward who runs from battle, and is shot like a dog," was a comparison made by Joseph P. Barry, a Santa Rosa California attorney, as he delivered an address during which he outlined in no uncertain terms "the American idea of Americans." It was said that Berry reflected the view of every Chico, California patriot in his arraignment of those wealthy individuals who could buy Liberty bonds but would not.[50]

During the last week of the Fourth Liberty Loan drive, an editor in Kentucky said Montgomery County was a fair bit away from its quota, as was the county on its War Savings Stamps quota. "This is due to the fact that we have a number of well-to-do men in our midst who have so far refused to buy a bond, buy any War Savings Stamps or contribute a cent to any Red Cross drive or similar movement...Just what ought to be done with such selfish slackers we are at a loss to know." He then cited Dr. Ganfield, who said, in a recent speech, "In times of peace, the county belongs to the people; it times of war, the people belong to the county." The editor agreed and felt the same held for property and declared that every man ought to respond in proportion to his abilities, "Unless he does he is not a good citizen and ought to be held up to public scorn." In a concluding warning he asserted that his newspaper "has always stood for law and order. It does not countenance force or intimidation at any time, but we want to warn those who have so far dodged their plain duty, that they are treading on dangerous ground. They are known and unless they redeem themselves in the eyes of the public by coming forward and buying their share of government securities, they will have only themselves to blame if their patriotic neighbors follow the example of several other counties and take matters into their own hands."[51]

Chapter 4. Commercial Tie-ins, Frauds, the Wealthy.

The sales hype surrounding the Liberty bonds spilled over into commercial entities of the time, trying to take advantage of that situation and to tie in their own company's product and services with the bonds by inserting something about the Liberty campaigns into their sales pitches. Thus they hoped to see their sales increase because of this supposed tie-in between the bond campaigns and their own companies. A more blatant commercial interest lay in the outright fraud that was also practiced to some extent as some sought, through illegal means, to benefit from all the hype and hysteria. Then there were the very wealthy buyers, or did they purchase bonds? Some articles spoke of committees that went after well-to-do people in their communities. Still, the concept of wealth was never defined precisely. Nor was it likely those wealthy people chased by committees were very wealthy in any objective sense. Such people may have been rich by the standards of their small communities, but on a larger, more national stage, they were perhaps not wealthy. But did the really wealthy such as Rockefeller, Carnegie, Frick, Armour, Ford, Vanderbilt, and so forth, buy Liberty bonds? Only on the rarest occasions did anyone in the media deal with that subject.

Commercial tie-ups were a regular feature of advertisements for a host of products. One such ad was for Waterman's pens. It urged the reader to sign up immediately for Liberty bonds and, when they did so, to fill out the paperwork using a Waterman's Ideal Fountain Pen. Another ad in a different newspaper on the same day was from Sone & Thomas, a department store chain based in Wheeling, West Virginia. In addition to its list of sale prices for various clothing items, it featured a separate box titled "Lend Him a Hand," with a sketch of a soldier. In that final week of a Liberty bond campaign, readers were commanded to "Get after the slacker. Search him out and help him to be a man and take a man's part in the war."[1]

An advertisement placed by a Greeneville, Tennessee retailer of men's and women's clothing featured at the head of the ad admonitions to buy Liberty bonds and a warning – "Don't be a Slacker."[2]

An ad placed by Lehn & Frank, maker of Pebeco toothpaste and Lysol disinfectant, bore the title, with respect to buying Liberty bonds – "Make no excuse – hear no excuse." This piece contained lengthy text that advised the reader to subscribe to the Fourth Liberty Loan bonds. "Do not lend your ear in encouraging attention to the excuse of the local slacker. Tell him to write out his poor meager defense on a piece of paper and send it to his children after the war," stated the advertisement. "As for the rare individual who buys no bonds at all, tell him to go and offend the ears of someone else with his absurd and insincere arguments." By purchasing bonds, one discouraged declared the piece, "the pitiful mouthings of the non-buyer who seeks from you some word of endorsement for his sorry failure to carry his share of the load."[3]

Heald's Business College in Sacramento, California, placed a small advertisement that decried "Mr. Bond Slacker." It went on to declare that; "Men and women of wealth are slackers of the worst type...Don't think that your neighbors are ignorant of your doings, for they are not. Public opinion is on your trail."[4]

A Wall Street firm named C. H. Venner & Company, 10 Wall Street, urged people to buy Liberty bonds. It advised people to purchase bonds to not less than 20 percent of the value of their property. Included was a handy chart to guide the readers; if a person was worth $10,000, then that person should hold at least $2,000 in Liberty bonds. For a person with $100,000 in property, then the bond holdings should be $20,000, and so forth. Emphasized was that bonds could be purchased with as little as 10 percent down, with the balance being borrowed from the bank. "After the war they will command a premium," stated the piece illogically, with no details provided. Since they offered a rate of interest slightly less than the going rate of those bonds, if sold before maturity, whether during the war or after it was over, they should have sold at a slight discount. The ad wondered, with regard to the purchase or not of Liberty bonds, "Am I a good citizen and entitled to the protection of the best Government on earth?"[5]

An advertisement in a New York City newspaper from the Loft candy company gave the various candy specials from the firm then on sale. Near the top of the ad was a declaration that "The Kaiser loves a Liberty loan 'slacker' like a brother, but he hates Liberty Bond buyers worse than double-barreled shotguns."[6]

A Phoenix, Arizona, car dealership placed an ad that referenced the treatment handed out to C. Reas, who a mob had badly abused for not buying bonds, and noted that what happened to Reas was all because he wouldn't buy a bond. The ad suggested, concerning bond purchases, that there should be "unconditional surrender for the bankroll." The page containing this ad held nothing but ads, about ten of them, and all focused on the subject of buying bonds and more bonds.[7]

There were not many outright commercial frauds that attached themselves to the Liberty Loan campaigns, at least not many that found their way into the media. One of them began with an involuntary petition in bankruptcy that was filed in federal court in New York City on November 16, 1917, against Elmer Dwiggins, a promoter with something called the "United States Government Liberty Loan Club," through which it was alleged that thousands of dollars were collected from small investors on the dollar-a-week plan for the Second Liberty Loan issue. Dwiggins was arrested on

November 16 in Montgomery, Alabama, on charges of misuse of the mail.[8]

A report a few days later clarified some of the details. In one account, Dwiggins was arrested on the night of November 15th. He was described as the manager of the New York agency of a Des Moines, Iowa, insurance company. Dwiggins explained that his troubles began when he started taking payments on bonds and investing them in securities on the New York Stock Exchange and that he lost about $100,000 when the market declined. At that point, he fled New York City and traveled to Montgomery, Alabama. Among the people whom he scammed money out of were said to be women and children. Dwiggins was alleged to have represented that the club through which he operated was an agency of the federal government. When Dwiggins' wife became convinced he had been defrauding women and children, she aided the officials in locating him, declaring that she was a patriot first and then a wife.[9]

On November 22, Dwiggins was indicted by the Federal grand jury on a charge of using the mail to defraud. That indictment was based on accusations made by Assistant United States Attorney Ben A. Mathews. He was charged with "knowingly, skillfully, unlawfully and feloniously devising a scheme and artifice to defraud divers persons;" the indictment consisted of seven counts. He was the former representative in New York City of the Bankers' Life Insurance Company of Des Moines. It was charged that 8,000 people had been affected by the manipulations of Dwiggins; seven of them were named in the indictment, one of which was a police officer. The maximum prison time upon conviction was five years on one count. Using a court order, federal agents opened his safety deposit box on November 21. They found that $7,000 in Liberty bonds had been removed since they examined the box the Saturday before Dwiggins left New York City for the South. When he was arrested in Montgomery, he had $6,800 worth of bonds with him.

At the time of the first inspection, $21,450 worth of Liberty bonds were found in the safety deposit box. However, Dwiggins argued that another person besides himself had a key to the box. At this point, it was estimated that his financial shortage then aggregated to $150,000. Of that amount, it was believed that nearly $81,000 applied to installments received from investors in Liberty bonds, who paid small amounts as down payments for the installment plan.[10]

On December 28, 1917, in New York City, Elmer Dwiggins pleaded guilty to the charges against him. He was sentenced to three years in the Atlanta penitentiary. In asking for a severe sentence, the Assistant United States District Attorney told federal Judge Learned Hand that the crimes of Dwiggins had bordered on treason because the frauds "tended to interfere with the successful prosecution of the war." However, the sentence handed down was relatively light.[11]

A New York City newspaper devoted an entire page to articles urging readers to buy Liberty bonds. That was early in April 1918 at the opening of the Third Liberty Loan drive. One of those articles was negative, as opposed to the effusively, relentlessly cheerful articles that comprised the rest of that page. That negative article was about what the reporter called "scalping" of the bonds, "profiteering in patriotism." Said the journalist, "It is a business that is all profit, with no possibility of a loss unless the Germans should capture the United States and convert it into a German colony." For some time past, the article explained, little ads had appeared in the "Help Wanted" columns of certain New York City newspapers offering spot cash for installment receipts on Liberty bonds. Those ads were calculated to appeal to people who subscribed for the First or Second Liberty bonds on the installment plan and then had, for some reason, been unable to meet all the subsequent payments, "They are planned to catch the eyes of men and women whose patriotism is more securely established than their financial position." People who, perhaps, had lost their jobs, became ill since signing up or had been struck by other misfortunes that necessitated extra expenses. Anyone who needed cash in a hurry and possessed receipts for part payment on loans to Uncle Sam was a potential candidate for these schemes. At the publicity bureau of the Liberty Loan Committee, it was stated that the United States government had no power to prosecute speculators in war bonds. A spokesman for the committee said it had sent representatives to all speculators "who had come to its notice" to "dissuade" them from continuing their business. That method was said to be inadequate as several scalpers' ads appeared in the want ad section of the *World* newspaper in the Sunday morning edition on April 7, 1918. All of those ads appeared under the general classification of "Help Wanted – Male" classification. Three examples were given in the article, minus the names and addresses of the advertisers, "Liberty bonds and installment receipts cashed immediately. Highest prices paid," "Liberty bonds or installments turned into cash immediately; open till 7 p.m; Sundays 10-1." and "Liberty bonds turned into spot cash without red tape. Apply Sundays, 11 a.m. to 3 p.m."[12]

According to the Liberty Loan Committee, the installment receipts were worth proportionately what the bonds were worth in the market – the price of bonds then being resold ranged from 96 to 98 percent of face value; that is, a bond owner who sold his $100 bond (years before its maturity) could expect to receive anywhere from $96 to $98, in the open market. A journalist went underground and made the rounds and called on one of the bond scalpers and told him he had subscribed for three $100 bonds of the First issue and had been able to pay only $75 of the total price. The scalper listed various expenses and fees before telling the reporter he would give him $45 for his $75 equity. Back at Liberty Loan headquarters, a spokesman considered that amount to be "liberal," with most people trying to sell their equity receiving only one-eighth to one-quarter of the value of their receipts. Thus, a man with $80 paid on a $100 bond was usually offered only from $10 to $20. The man with the $75 equity should have expected legitimately to receive from $72 to $73.50. Subscribers who had made partial payments and suddenly wanted out could have their money refunded from the government, "but this takes some time," and most victims of scalpers found themselves with an urgent need for immediate cash. Specific stores in New York City had advertised, relatively recently, that they would accept Liberty bonds in payment for goods the same as with gold or currency. United States Treasury Secretary William McAdoo stopped that practice merely by appealing to businessmen not to treat the bonds as currency. New York County District Attorney Edward Swan had taken up bond scalping to prevent speculation. Assistant District Attorney Edward S. Brogan of the commercial frauds department said he had been looking into the matter and that his office would bring whatever legal pressure to bear that could be applied against the men profiteering in Liberty bonds.[13]

One day later, the Liberty Loan Committee in New York City created what it felt was the first stumbling block in the path of the bond scalpers. It announced it was determined to protect subscribers to the Third issue from "leeches who speculate in the misfortunes of others and relieve them of gilt-edged securities at a ruinous discount." If scalping was not checked by the publicity given to the practice, then the committee "may take steps to make speculation in the first and second war issues a real hazard, with small opportunities for profit and a good chance for getting into trouble with the United States Secret Service." The committee announced that at the central installment payment bureau in New York City, subscribers to the Third bond issue would have an opportunity to sell their bonds if they could not afford to continue their installment payments. Thus, in New York City, there were 600 stations where the subscriber could make his installment payments. Still, there would be only one station where he could arrange to sell his bond if he found it financially necessary. At the end of the article, the journalist noted, "The war bond scalping business is evidently growing. Four scalpers advertised yesterday in the morning papers."[14]

To protect Liberty Loan subscribers from scalpers who had been buying up small bond holdings at reduced prices, New York City's Nathan Straus announced, in April 1918, that he was organizing a society to take over the bonds at par from such holders as had an immediate need of their money. Straus was well-known in New York City as one of the owners of two of the city's huge department stores, R. H. Macy and Company and Abraham & Straus. He announced his plan before a large crowd. He declared that he would advance $25,000 of his own money and believed several other wealthy individuals in the city would contribute an equal amount toward a fund to take over relinquished bonds. Straus believed that profiteers who speculated in bonds could be driven out of business if the investors could cash their bonds at par. Said a reporter; "It is his plan to investigate all cases where money is sought for the bonds and to confine financial assistance to worthy cases."[15]

While minor alterations in the system were, perhaps, implemented, the problem of scalpers remained and resurfaced occasionally. "In view of the many misunderstandings and the great amount of trickery growing out of the sale and resale of Liberty bonds the Liberty Loan Committee has found it necessary to establish a complaint bureau at 120 Broadway [New York City] where small investors or those in doubt as to matters in connection with their bonds will be given proper information." It was acknowledged that many complaints were received at the offices of the Loan Committee; "In many instances it has been found that tricksters deliberately have taken advantage of the small investors' ignorance on bond matters. Many subscribers had never dealt in securities before and bought a portion of the loan for patriotic reasons. Some have been forced to sell, and financial sharks have in many instances deliberately gulled the seller."[16]

One week later, New York Assistant District Attorney Brogan announced his office had launched a crusade against Liberty bond scalpers. Some of the scalpers were reported to have persuaded bond owners to part with their bonds for less than market prices. The Capital Issues Committee had asked Brogan for a list of 50 alleged "wildcat" brokers under subpoena charged with inducing investors to part with their Liberty bonds. This article admitted concerning scalpers inducing investors to sell for less than market prices "by using arguments which, although perhaps inside the law, reflect seriously on the desirability of the bonds as investments." Brogan was said to have notified those scalpers that they were expected to contribute to the Loan Committee an amount of advertising space equal to that ordinarily used in advertising offers to buy Liberty bonds and to discontinue their activities until the $6 billion target goal of the Fourth Liberty Loan drive had been attained.[17]

A month after that, it was reported that advertisements that appeared in a morning newspaper in New York City on October 28, 1918, offering to buy bonds of the Fourth issue or paid-up installments on such bonds, or to lend money on the bonds at six percent interest, were taken as an indication that the bond scalpers were as avid for the Fourth issue bonds as for those of the previous issues. Reportedly, the Liberty Loan Committee was set to launch a counter-offensive in the form of an education campaign to inform bondholders that many banks had offered to make loans up to 90 percent of the face value of the bond and at an interest rate of 4.25 percent. District Attorney Brogan stood ready, it was said, to investigate all complaints regarding scalpers who were then offering only 20 percent to 75 percent of equity on all the bond issues.[18]

In April 1919, by order of United States Treasury Secretary Carter Glass, thousands of posters warning people against Liberty Loan scalpers were issued by the outdoor division of the publicity department of the Liberty Loan Committee. That move was taken as part of the campaign against "unscrupulous dealers" who had been victimizing holders of Liberty bonds. The posters contained the following notice; "For Your Protection. Read." And stated in the body of the poster, "Dishonest men are tempting people to exchange their Liberty Bonds and invest their hard-earned savings in get-rich-quick schemes that promise big returns, but are worthless. Hold fast to your Liberty Bonds. Don't exchange them for anything. Don't sell them unless absolutely necessary. Keep them in a safe place or have them registered, free, in your name." [Yet only bonds of $5,000 and up were registered automatically at the time of issue].[19]

That same month the Federal Trade Commission in Washington was in the midst of an investigation of bond scalpers' and stock jobbers' activities. Said a journalist; "If any person – man or woman – offers you a stock or security in exchange for your Liberty Bonds get that person's name and all the 'literature' offered and mail them to the Commission."[20]

Those recommendations designed to curb scalpers in Liberty bonds and profiteers defrauding investors in the government loans were made to Carter Glass by Edward S. Brogan, New York Assistant District Attorney, who headed the bureau of commercial frauds at the District Attorney's office. He explained that an investigation initiated by Brogan more than one year earlier resulted in the nationwide movement to stamp out such profiteering. If his earlier advice had been taken, "millions of dollars would have been saved by investors." Said Brogan; On April 6, 1918, during the Third Liberty Loan campaign, "I protested against the plans of publishing lists of subscribers in towns and villages, because unscrupulous promoters would obtain thousands of names to circularize for the purpose of exchanging worthless stocks for Liberty bonds." And, he continued, "I urged the necessity of mailing a small pamphlet to such subscribers warning them against surrendering their bonds without complete investigation and notifying some national, state or county official of any attempt to defraud them." Publicity, education, and "sane legislation" were necessary, said Brogan. He then referred to another type of profiteer, the Liberty bond scalpers. From a mere handful, those concerns had increased until now; hundreds were operating in New York City alone, and "probably thousands throughout the country." They simply hung out signs anywhere, calling themselves "Liberty bond brokers." They paid very low rates on the bond equity offered by sellers. Brogan urged that publicity be kept up after the Victory loan drive ended, stating, "The prices during the last six months are ridiculously low and are no doubt proving a source of trouble in disparaging of the Victory bonds to poorer people."[21]

Wealthy people were not often mentioned when it came to the Liberty bonds campaigns. Occasionally an article spoke about some rich person, in various parts of the country, being pursued, or named, or shamed for lack of proper participation in the program. However, those people may have been wealthy in their relatively small communities. Wealth, of course, was never defined. Concerning the very wealthy in America, that group was mentioned even less frequently in the Third Liberty Loan. Of the 18 million Americans who subscribed, all except 22,500 bought bonds ranging from $50 to $10,000. Only those 22,500 (and that number included corporations) bought bonds to an amount over $10,000. Said the United States Treasury Secretary William McAdoo; "It would be preposterous to say that there are only 22,500 men, women and corporations in America able to lend more than $10,000 each to their government on Liberty bonds." McAdoo added that the record of the Third Liberty Loan; "conclusively shows that the great mass of the American people, the men and women of small and moderate means, were highly patriotic and did their duty splendidly whereas only 22,500 persons and corporations among America's wealthier classes bought bonds above the $10,000 mark...these figures at least indicate that they did not respond to the call of the government in the Third Liberty Loan commensurately with their ability to help." An earnest appeal was made to that class for them to do more in the Fourth Liberty Loan. McAdoo also suggested what was needed was a more "effective and intelligent" organizations of the bankers and Liberty Loan committees of the country to secure a secondary distribution of Liberty bonds and of stabilizing their value; that is, to set up a reasonably efficient resale method. McAdoo argued that we had to provide the machinery and the means to do so "and get the highest possible price for them, while at the same time protecting the innocent investor against swindlers and unscrupulous and unpatriotic people who, contrary to the earnest request of the Treasury Department, have induced holders of Liberty Bonds to exchange them for stocks or investments of dubious value." The effect of that was to force the Treasury to buy the Liberty bonds which these "unscrupulous and unpatriotic" people acquired and threw upon the market. It has to take part of the money it had borrowed from the public and buy back those Liberty bonds to protect the market and the credit of the government. McAdoo stressed the government had no objection to the sale of those bonds, where imperative, "but we should constantly appeal to the intelligent self-interest and patriotism of those who buy Liberty bonds to keep them to the utmost limit of their ability as one of the sacred duties they have to perform in this war."[22]

On the west coast, chairman C. S. Wills of the King County Washington Liberty Loan campaign declared that the small investor was doing his part but that the businessman and the wealthy citizen were failing to respond. Said Wills, "The wealthy citizens and the large business firms of Seattle are not subscribing the quotas assigned to them and in some cases these people are not even showing the proper respect to the solicitors. Drastic action will be taken, if need be, to force these shirkers to do their part." Reportedly, with this announcement of shirkers, "a recombing is under way in many industrial plants, and solicitors are taking up new subscriptions from business and financial men who previously tendered checks below their quotas." Despite the article lead-in that suggested the wealthy were the laggards and the small investor was doing his part, much of this article concentrated on those little guys. The reporter ended his account by remarking that one of the first industrial plants to start a new drive was that of the Patterson-MacDonald shipyard, where hundreds of employees already had taken out bond subscriptions.[23]

An article published in the early stages of the Fourth Liberty Loan drive complained about the slow response to that campaign. It then remarked that the campaign aimed at wealthy people who had not taken their proportionate share of bonds was started a day earlier at a meeting held at the Chamber of Commerce in New York City where 250 members of the New York Stock Exchange, who had volunteered to round up the Liberty bond slackers, received instructions from Seward Prosser, president of the Bankers Trust Company and chairman of the committee appointed to conduct that roundup. When he discussed the aims of the campaign targeting the wealthy, Benjamin Strong, chairman of the Liberty Loan Committee and Governor of the Federal Reserve Bank of New York, stated, "We have not only to carry our own burden but a large part of the burden of our allies. This city cannot afford to, will not and must not fail to raise the amount of money asked for by the Government as its quota." Strong added, "The work of raising this sum is laid out among an army of workers, but there is one class that can best be reached by a personal and intensive canvass by men of standing such as you. I refer to those people of large means and independent income." Their position differed significantly from that of the laboring men, Strong informed his wealthy audience, "who as a class have responded magnificently to the appeal to buy bonds, but this class of men, the laboring men, have nothing to fall back on in case they lose their jobs or become ill. On the other hand, the rich men, the men of large means and assured income, which they receive whether they work or not, are a class that can with greater certainty mortgage their future than can any other class in the country, even more so than the corporations. It is the most important task in this city to get these men to subscribe their quota. It may prove an unpleasant task in some cases." Present at the event was banker J. P. Morgan, who told the crowd that he did not know how to approach those wealthy men who had not taken their fair share "but that unless it was done systematically and thoroughly it could not be done."[24]

A few days later, an account appeared on the other side of America, published in a California newspaper. That article revolved around the failure of "wealthy residents" of the Chico, California area to subscribe to the Fourth Liberty Loan to the degree that they should have subscribed. At a meeting of the local committee, it was decided to publish the names of "all rich persons" who failed to buy their share of bonds. As soon as arrangements could be perfected, it was reported, a list containing the names of wealthy men and women slackers would be turned over to "competent judges" who would determine the amount they should have subscribed to, along with the amount that they did buy, and that information would be given to the press for immediate publication. Said a spokesman for that local committee; "Certain individuals are failing in their patriotic duty to lend the government their money willingly, and it is the purpose of this committee to see that persons who hand in $1,000 subscriptions when they should subscribe $10,000 or more are made known to the general public.[25]

When United States Treasury Secretary William McAdoo spoke in Baltimore during the Fourth Liberty Loan drive, he pointed out that the businessmen – men with ample means – had not subscribed to the extent they should have to the previous loans. He urged "men of moderate means and men of larger means" to use their credit, saying that United States President Woodrow Wilson had set an example by taking $20,000 of the bonds on the installment plan. McAdoo again mentioned that during the Third issue, only 22,500 subscribers out of the total of 18 million purchasers of bonds had bought to the extent of $10,000 or more. "This is a very poor showing," said McAdoo, and only a "small percentage" of the large corporations in the country bought more than $10,000 worth of bonds during that campaign. Concluded the Secretary; "The men who were able to subscribe large amounts didn't come in. But we have the goods on them now, and they must come up this time."[26]

Chapter 5. Investigations.

Although the selling blitz and the hype surrounding the need for bonds, the need for everyone to buy them, and so forth, was intense and attained levels rarely seen for a government program, it was not enough. An intense effort was launched against anyone who refused and resisted the relentless pressure to buy, to ensure total compliance and conformity to the need to have the lower classes pay for the war in blood and money. The most draconian measures were the physical beatings and thuggery visited on many victims. Somewhat less severe was the practice of naming and shaming those who refused to buy or who bought less than the ruling classes had dictated as the proper amount. The third and least draconian measure was generally applied first. That was the investigation of citizens who were not above suspicion. It involved the hapless victims who refused to buy bonds being hauled before committee after committee to be hounded, hectored, and badgered until they finally gave up and subscribed to buy bonds. One of the earliest of those investigations was launched just after the official end of the First Liberty Loan drive. It was reported from Chicago that Liberty bond slackers of that city might as well "surrender gracefully." That was because the Federal Reserve Bank had just announced that 500 life insurance agents had started after them.[1]

One of the investigations did not go after the slackers but targeted the sellers of the bonds. The federal government's Internal Revenue Service sent one of its officials, W. F. Chambers, to Omaha to investigate local conditions that had arisen from the recent bond sale campaign in which people had complained that the banks and members of the soliciting committees were receiving a 10 percent commission on the sale of the Liberty bonds. All such sales were supposed to be free of all commissions or other fees. Nothing more was reported on this case.[2]

Early in the Third Liberty bond campaign, it was reported that the government had sent an "army of registered men, under precinct captains," to ask questions of the head of each family in Seattle. Questions to be asked included; "Have you bought a Third Liberty Loan bond?" "Do you intend to buy one?" and "If not, why not?" Cards "filed away for government reference" would contain the record of each man's financial part in the war. The work had been quietly going on for several days, and by the end of the week, that data was expected to be in the hands of federal officials. And "A check will then follow, to see if the answers are correct." When a man said he did not intend to buy a bond, the agents were required to obtain a written statement of his reasons. Spaces were also provided on the cards to record any purchases of War Savings Stamps by the person and for any donations to organizations engaged in war work, such as Red Cross. The Seattle Liberty Loan committee was working toward a benchmark of one subscriber for every five individuals in the city.[3]

Farmers were accused as a class of being bond slackers in a bulletin mailed throughout the Seventh Federal Reserve District (all of Iowa and most of Illinois, Indiana, Michigan, and Wisconsin) by the Liberty Loan Committee. That bulletin alleged that farmers under-subscribed their share of the First and Second loans, even though "enormous profits" had been assured to them along with a "light" tax burden. It did not hesitate to call the agriculturalist a profiteer, stating he got 56 percent more for his meat, 77 percent more for garden and dairy products, and 86 percent more for other products. Foodstuffs, said the bulletin, had advanced 146 percent in price since 1914, while the price of metals had increased by only 82 percent while other staples, outside of food, had risen just 53 percent. Such figures argued the bulletin removed any talk about industrial profiteering, and the farmers continued the bulletin "escape 90 per cent of the income tax."[4]

Having charge of the Liberty Loan program, the United States Treasury Department requested and demanded that all names of all persons financially able to buy Liberty bonds and who did not be reported to the State chairmen, who, in turn, would report them to the Treasury Department in Washington. It was reported that in Washington, a list would be prepared of all people who purchased bonds, and they would be listed in a card index as "American Citizens. Those who refused to buy would be listed as "Slackers," and their names would be turned over to the Council of Defense for action. The country's banks had agreed to loan 90 percent of the purchase price of the bonds at six percent interest, holding the bonds as collateral security; "If you have not the ready money to buy bonds, you are expected to loan the Government your credit." Concluded a journalist, "You have no excuse for not buying Liberty Bonds, for there is none. If you do not want your name placed in the card index in the Treasury Department as a Slacker, then buy a Liberty Bond in proportion to your financial condition." And, he added, "Do not try to camouflage your patriotism by buying a hundred dollar bond when you should buy a thousand dollar bond. Do your part. Let there be not any slackers in Bates County [Missouri]."[5]

One article that discussed the federal government's announced intention to compile a list of slackers said that persons who were "financially unable" to buy bonds would not be listed "or be embarrassed in any way by the index of names of persons who are able but not willing to aid the government in the present crisis." However, many other articles argued that no excuses existed not to buy bonds or were acceptable. Township chairmen of the loan committees were asked to report the names of the slackers, and the list "will be carefully gone over by the county committee to see that no injustice is done to anybody." A committee would then visit the men listed by the township officials. If they still refused, their names would be reported to the Federal Reserve director of bond sales.[6]

In Bernalillo County, New Mexico, a reporter informed readers that the area's Liberty bond drive had made "elaborate preparations" to get after the loan slackers. The names of some 4,000 citizens of Bernalillo County, heads of families, and other adults had been card indexed. That work continued for two months before the Third Liberty Loan drive started. Those cards had all been sorted, and the officials determined that those who did not buy bonds and those who did not buy enough would get "further attention" from the bond solicitors.[7]

A general article published during the Third Liberty Loan drive lamented the fact that sales were lagging and not moving as fast or as well as expected; that such lagging was especially true in the large cities. Those bond drives were often pitched in the media as a race; that is, which city was first, which county was first, which state, and so on. For example, the New York district was said to be in fifth place, with about 33 percent of the area's quota being subscribed. It was also noted that; "Efforts are being made by the loan directors to have complete reports as to the number of individual subscribers obtained in each district. This is looked upon as the best method of determining where the bond slackers are located."[8]

In Spokane, Washington, after a committee of citizens interested in soliciting Liberty bonds had appeared before the United States District Attorney Garrecht in April 1918, deputy marshals were sent in quest of seven people alleged to have refused to purchase bonds. However, it was said they were amply able to do so. Those seven cases were then brought before the Federal grand jury. Those questioned were L. B. Whitten, A. A. Barnett, Valentine Reynolds, Maurice S. Lindholm, John P. Brawl, Stewart Drelbelits, and Herman Linke. Following their appearance before U.S. Marshall James McGovern, after they had been reported as bond slackers, Whitten and Barnett made "substantial" purchases of the Third Liberty Loan issue. Whitten subscribed for $1,100 of bonds, and Barnett took $500. Reynolds bought a $50 bond. The grand jury took no action in any of these seven cases, with federal officials expressing that there was no legal method by which the men could be prosecuted.[9]

In Barber County, Kansas, the yellow tag to identify slackers was said to be working. Every Liberty bond slacker was listed with the loan committee for that area, preserving his name on a yellow card, "and his standing is established for all time. That is the program of the 'strong arm' and 'yellow dog' committee in the county..." according to J. N. Tincher, a well-known lawyer who resided in Medicine Lodge Kansas. A few days earlier, Tincher and several Medicine Lodge businessmen were soliciting bond subscriptions. One farmer said he would buy $100 worth of bonds. As a subscription was about to be written, Tincher said, "Hold on, this man will do his part or nothing." The record of the farmer's crop and livestock sales was produced, and the subscription was "boosted several hundred percent." Said Tincher, "When we find a man who hesitates or quibbles, we look up his financial record if any phase of it is not clear. Then he is told just what is expected. We don't compromise when it comes to putting up money with which to win this war."[10]

There was said to be a strong sentiment in Durant, Oklahoma, at the end of the Third Liberty Loan drive to expose slackers through "wide publicity" to the public's attention. Then the local committee, plus the Council of Defense, were expected to take some action against slackers when the campaign officially ended. Remarked a journalist, "When the campaign here is ended, each subscriber's name probably will be published with the amount of his subscription."[11]

At the request of the Liberty Loan committee of the Second Federal Reserve District (encompassing all of New York State, some of northern New Jersey, and a few other areas), one of New York City's departments began an investigation of the more than 30,000 signers of bond subscription forms who had failed to follow through on those pledges and buy those bonds. City employees had reportedly seen "a number of the signers and obtained from them statements as to their reasons for declining to take the bonds for which they subscribed." To that point, the investigation showed that; "a good percentage of them have made some payments on their subscriptions and that others are willing to do so. Still, others explained they had bought bonds through other channels. About one-quarter of the names investigated so far have not been traced.[12]

The Third Liberty Loan Committee in Ogden, Utah, was engaged, in June 1918, in carefully checking, sifting, and listing the names of those citizens of Weber County, Utah, who purchased bonds during the campaign, which had officially closed a few weeks earlier. Assessment rolls and "other data" had been checked to ascertain "as accurately as possible the ability of citizens to purchase, by comparison, to see if all individuals purchased to the extent of their ability." After completing the checking and comparison, those persons who, in the committee's judgment, did not come forward to the extent of their ability will have their names placed on lists, and "it is presumed the lists will be turned over to government agents. It is very likely that the federal agents will then take some action regarding the matter."[13]

Concerning that exercise in Ogden, a few days later, it was reported that those committeemen doing the investigations had discovered some signed up for the various Liberty bond drives. Still, when the time came to pay for their pledges, those people had not made good. As a result, the investigators were threatening to publish "a list of the evaders of this great public duty," and that this would be done even though among the delinquents "are men of high standing in this community." Concluded a journalist, "This is a war in which no one can be allowed to do less than his utmost. The man who is well-to-do must contribute in proportion to his wealth, and he must not be allowed to gain the notion that, if he does not do all that is possible, some other more willing, generous soul will accept his burden and carry it."[14]

The idea of investigating and listing financial slackers extended beyond the Liberty bonds to the part of the Red Cross engaged in war work and to the War Savings Stamps program. According to a report from Kentucky, persons who did not own and refused to purchase War Savings Stamps would be recorded on yellow cards along with the reason for the refusal and to be available and open to public inspection. Such a movement was said to be state-wide across Kentucky, and all county chairmen of the various committees would be supplied with the cards. "The purchase of Liberty Loans, the contributions to the Red Cross and to the War Chest, are not an excuse for a failure to buy War Savings Stamps," declared a memo from officials. A house-to-house canvass was to be made by the committee and its sales force of solicitors.[15]

The executive committee of the local chapter of the Red Cross in Glasgow, Montana, reported that it had received information that there were a large number of people living in Valley County, Montana, who were financially well able to help in the war effort by subscribing to the Red Cross but who were not giving any money whatsoever for Red Cross purposes. The committee felt that a person who was able to contribute to the Red Cross but did not was "either a slacker or a pro-German, and they have begun a process for the purpose of weeding out that class of people and giving to them the publicity which they deserve." Lists of names were then in the process of being checked, "and when the non-subscribers are listed, a proper committee will call on them to see that they either perform their duty to the county by subscribing to the Red Cross, or accept the consequences of being shunned by the patriotic citizens of the county."[16]

Following the receipt of information to the effect that some persons who make pledges and signed notes for monthly payments for the support of the local Red Cross work were failing to make good their promises, the Grady County Oklahoma Council of Defense, at one of its regular meetings of the executive committee, passed a resolution asking the Red Cross chapter for a complete report on such "delinquents." It was decided to summon all who had failed to make their payments before the council, and they would be asked to show cause why they should not be placed on the "slacker list." Two months later, this group declared that a "Slacker Drive" would be started within two or three days, according to J. W. Keyser, an official with the county Red Cross. Every slacker was said to be the object of the drive to compel slackers to make good on their failed promises.[17]

The Boone County Missouri Council of Defense sent out forms requesting information about "financial slackers," people who had not contributed or had contributed "very little" in proportion to their means to war relief funds and government bond issues. They received nine replies, including, "A whole school district has been charged by one informant with not supporting the Government." A committee was to be appointed to deal with those reported cases. People deemed financial slackers were to be allowed to subscribe for War Savings Certificates, join the Red Cross "and in other ways to help the Government. Letters will be sent to them telling them that they have been reported to the council. Members of the council think that in many cases this will be sufficient," to cause the people being investigated to take the necessary steps to remove themselves from the slacker list. The names of the informants were not released, and the plan of the Council of Defense was to keep all the information it received as confidential, but if the reported slackers did not contribute, "their neighbors will be informed."[18]

In April 1918, it was reported that a Tulsa, Oklahoma, millionaire had recently moved to Kansas City, Missouri, to "avoid doing his duty to his country by contributing to war funds and buying Liberty bonds – and they're going to make him come across with some of his thousands." A day earlier, the chairman of the Kansas City Liberty bond campaign called A. V. Davenport, city manager of the Tulsa campaign, and asked for the Kansas City address of the "self expatriated slacker." Davenport provided the address, and it was said, "those Kansas City bond salesmen are going to make the gentleman respond or make it so hot for him that he'll move on to another city." The millionaire referred to had most of his holdings in Tulsa. His income, from rent alone, was estimated at $50,000 a year. Yet, he had contributed only about $400 to all war funds combined and purchased one $1,000 Liberty bond. Said Davenport; "He is a class A-1 first, 18-carat slacker..." It was alleged that local war workers agreed he had moved to Kansas City to avoid buying Liberty bonds. He was then in a city where he and his wealth were unknown, which led him to believe; "he would not be bothered by persistent soliciting," as had happened with the Tulsa workers who were well acquainted with his financial wealth. So those workers immediately notified the managers of the Kansas City war workers to locate him and make him "come across."[19]

The general committee for Marshall County, Iowa, in charge of the Liberty Loan campaign for that area, met as a "board of equalization" to review the allotments made by the various ward committees and then made changes in the quota amounts assigned to 47 bond subscribers and, it was reported; "that will increase the bond subscription for the city." After the bond sale, those who failed to clear their accounts satisfactorily to their ward chairmen would be certified to the Iowa Council of Defense for investigation as to their loyalty. Noted a reporter; "If they fail to be acquitted upon fair trial they will be certified to the treasury department at Washington as slackers, yellow cards for that purpose having been furnished by the department. These cards will then be turned over to federal officers."[20]

The Lake County Indiana Council of Defense got after Liberty Loan slackers at the beginning of October 1918 and had some well-to-do Lake County men on the "hot seat" for some time. "The interviews between the defense council and these men netted bond sales of nearly $5,000, according to a news account. On the following day, a number of other people were to be investigated with one of them described as "a prominent Hammond [IN] man, who is estimated to be worth $100,000, has two motor cars, spends his winters in Florida, and in all the four Liberty Loans has paid $10 on a $100 bond." He had also repeatedly ignored summons to appear before members of Hammond's bond officials. To explain his attitude, this unnamed individual was again ordered to appear before the committee. More sessions of the Lake County Council of Defense were held a couple of weeks later, and much of the time was used by those cited to explain why they had not bought Liberty bonds. To that point, the council had ruled against publishing the names of those cited before the body for failure to subscribe to the bond issue, "but there is a feeling throughout the county, especially in the north, that the practice obtaining in other councils of defense should be carried out in Lake County and that is to give the fullest publicity to these cases so that they may serve as a warning." Some who were summoned to appear before the council failed to do so, and the council promised to summon them again in the near future.[21]

In New York City, to go after those who signed pledges for the Fourth Liberty bond issue but "forgot" to make their initial payment showing their good faith – and many thousands of people did that in the Third Liberty bond issue – a committee known as the "Follow-up Committee" was appointed to induce the pledge-makers to make a first payment at once. That committee was chaired by J. W. Honor, who had called 1,000 men and women volunteers to round up all those bond slackers.[22]

When the Liberty Loan Board of Review in South Bend, Indiana, was sitting in a final judgment of slackers, it did so with a force of some 300 volunteer workers who were ready to begin a cleanup campaign on all cases where those involved had failed to purchase their full quota of bonds. The committee believed that just because 90 percent of the people of South Bend had done their whole duty, the remaining 10 percent should not be allowed to escape without having done their fair share. Each of the 300 workers had from 10 to 15 cards bearing the names of those who had failed to buy their full quota. Those people would be visited and asked why they failed to meet their quotas. No time was to be wasted, and if those visited did not show the "proper spirit," the committee would simply turn the cases over to the board of review. At its first such session, the board of review dealt with 50 cases. Twenty-five of those cases were "straightened out by the board," but there remained 25 cases for which summonses had been issued for the people to appear before the board; however, those 25 people had failed to attend those sessions.[23]

According to a journalist writing for an Oklahoma newspaper, "Liberty Loan slackers are to feel the weight of public indignation and even a more severe penalty, if necessary, to bring them to a realization of their duty." The executive committee for the Fourth Liberty Loan in that area was to hold a meeting to decide on the action to take and to "check over subscriptions. It is intended to check bond purchases against the known resources of the subscribers and those who are not bearing their full part will be investigated by the committee." The speculation was that the "Kansas City plan" would secure serious consideration, and many committee members favored it. Under that plan, names written on yellow cards were turned over to a "follow-up committee." Those cards listed the individual's financial rating and the amount of his subscription if any, "and then there is no dodging the facts during the 'follow-up' interview with the individual...Those who have bought much less than their assignments will find an adequate remedy in the hands of the committee and it is likely that many will hasten to add to their meager subscriptions."[24]

In Phoenix, Arizona, a reportedly "large number" of anonymous letters regarding bond slackers were being received at Liberty Loan headquarters at the Chamber of Commerce office. However, the committee had decided to ignore any such communications unless the letters were signed. A statement from the "shock committee," which investigated people who had not bought bonds in proportion to their ability to pay, said, "The committee expressed itself quite tolerant of religious opinions which constrain conscientious men from contributing in any wise to the prosecution of the war. It is not at all tolerant, however, of any opinions that would influence any resident of this community from doing his share in aid of the successful conclusion of this war who still remain in the community." Continued the statement, 'Any man who has conscientious religious objections to contributing to the support of the government in the prosecution of this war, must necessarily have conscientious scruples to being in this country. He can't honestly live in this country and refuse to support it." The committee went on to point out that its attention had been called to a number of people who gave as their excuse for not buying bonds that they had religious opinions opposed to war but were keen to secure to themselves "the utmost of the profits arising from war activities and who expect not only to have the benefit of those profits in the general prosperity of this country due to the war temporarily and the general prosperity that must inevitably follow the successful prosecution of the war." As far as the committee was concerned, if one was conscientiously opposed to the prosecution of the war and he was honest in that opinion; "there is but one alternative for him, and that is to leave the country and go to some country and become a citizen of it where war just or unjust, honorable or dishonorable, justified or unjustified, will not be waged." As a final thought, the committee declared, "Anybody having any information regarding any person who is able to buy bonds should turn such names and addresses in at headquarters in order that these cases may be brought before the committee."[25]

At a meeting of the Bates County Missouri Council of Defense, the matter of people refusing to buy Liberty bonds was taken up. It was moved and carried at that meeting that all bond solicitors report to the secretary or chairman of the County Council of Defense the names and addresses of all parties refusing to purchase bonds "in such amounts as the solicitors deem they should, and that this Council cite such parties to appear before this Council and show cause why he does not subscribe. Refusal to obey such citation will be taken by the Council as prima facie evidence of the party being a slacker."[26]

A "large number" of Liberty Loan slackers were summoned before the Council of Defense at Maysville, Kentucky, on October 18, 1918, to state their reasons for not purchasing bonds. Remarked a journalist; "After a brief discussion of the matter, when the advisability of such an investment was clearly defined the majority of the slackers were willing and glad to purchase bonds of the Fourth issue, and over $40,000 were sold."[27]

At the same time, Seattle, Washington, reported that it had reached its quota for the Fourth bond issue. One of the reasons it did so was its vigilance in "the smoking out of bond deserters..." And, "In a number of cases we had to send committee after committee to visit wealthy men who were holding back. To one man we sent three committees in succession. Each returned with a contribution of $500. Then we sent a fourth committee and this one returned with a check for $5,000. That man had at last subscribed his quota." It was also observed that; "In other cases we had to send as many as seven 'shock' committees to visit one individual. This ceaseless pounding has proved its worth."[28]

Redwood County Minnesota Attorney Emersen stated that the few bond slackers in that county were not yet through with the process. All of the evidence presented by those men in their hearings before the county executive committee was to be sent by Emersen to the Naturalization Department at Washington, and; "if found sufficient proof of bad citizenship, the citizenship papers of the men investigated will be revoked." Emersen claimed several such lawsuits had been started on those grounds in the eastern courts.[29]

"While the mere refusal to invest in Liberty Bonds is not an indictable offense, such a refusal from a man able to buy bonds is likely to have behind it some offense which does come within the federal laws." That was reported to be the belief of the United States Attorney for the northern district of Georgia [unnamed], who sent the following letter to W. C. Wardlaw, chair of the district Liberty Loan committee in Chapel Hill, North Carolina; "Referring to several cases which have been brought to my attention in which persons who are amply able to subscribe to bonds and refuse to do so, you are advised that the mere failure to take bonds, however unpatriotic it may be, is not in itself and when disconnected with other matters, an indictable offense." The US attorney added, "At the same time, experience has shown that people of this character can very frequently be indicted for other offenses. The man who has not sufficient patriotism to aid his country in this manner, will generally be found to have made expressions which tend to favor the cause of a government with which we are at war, or indicate opposition to the cause of our government therein. Matters of this sort are indictable, and the penalty may extend to imprisonment for thirty years and a fine of many thousands of dollars." He went on to suggest to Wardlaw, therefore, "that you cause the past record and conduct and utterances of the people of this class to be carefully investigated and reviewed in the communities where they respectively live, with a view of ascertaining whether they are not indictable under the espionage or sedition acts." And, he concluded in his letter to Wardlaw, "In all such cases the names and facts should be reported to the United States attorney in the districts where such objectionable people live. Juries are not only willing but anxious to convict in all such cases."[30]

It was announced in January 1919 that the names of persons who had not paid their War Savings Stamps pledges by February 1 would be posted on corners in the residential area where they lived; that is, they would if a plan proposed by a businessman was adopted. The scheme was then considered by War Savings bank officials. The original deadline for making good on those pledges was January 1; however, it was extended to February 1.[31]

Slackers during the Victory Loan (often called the Fifth Liberty Loan) drive were hauled before the local Council of Defense, according to C. L. Kennedy, chairman of the Brown County South Dakota Council of Defense. Kennedy said that while all the rules that governed the Councils of Defense during the war were then suspected – it was April 1919 – the council still planned to function during the Victory Loan campaign.[32]

Around the same time, the South Dakota State Council of Defense issued an order delegating authority to the chairman in each county to require any person to appear before him for examination and could require that person to state why he should or should not buy Liberty bonds. The circuit court said the order would issue a subpoena upon request of the chairman of the executive committee of the state council. Any person who refused to obey such a subpoena or answer any questions at the hearing would be punished for contempt of court.[33]

Chapter 6. Naming and Shaming.

One of the ways that society tried to bring the resisters into line and compel them to buy war bonds and not become or remain financial slackers, was by subjecting them to naming and shaming. Bond committees made many threats at the local or even the federal level to publish the names of all bond slackers in their area, usually in local newspapers. However, the threat was rarely carried out. It was more likely that the names of people who had purchased bonds (and sometimes the amount bought) were published instead. That method was a type of back door approach to the problem and allowed the reader to infer that any name not published on such a list was a slacker. Publishing a list of people defined as "slackers" perhaps opened that publication to lawsuits. While comprehensive lists of slackers were rarely published, what did often happen was that the names of one or two or a few people were listed along with all the facts showing the named example was indeed a shameful being, a slacker. This kind of shaming supposedly compelled the resisters to purchase bonds. More importantly, it set an example for anyone considering not purchasing war bonds.

October 24, 1917, was designated Liberty Day by US President Woodrow Wilson. Business was to be suspended, as far as possible, that day to concentrate on "patriotic demonstrations" and on efforts to sell Liberty bonds – the official end of the Second Liberty Loan drive was approaching. The local Liberty Loan Committee in Oklahoma City, Oklahoma, was one group that was worried that daily sales were not moving fast enough the meet that city's quota of $3,060,000 for that specific campaign. Much of the problem, thought the Oklahoma City committee, was that not enough volunteers had come forward to sell the bonds. Discussion on a solution for Oklahoma City then centered around abandoning the volunteer recruitment of "privates" in the bond-selling effort and, in some fashion, "drafting" them. Reportedly, Judge C. B. Ames, a member of the local Liberty Loan executive committee, had decided upon a policy of "pitiless publicity toward Liberty loan slackers," defined herein as men able to buy bonds yet who refused to do so; and men who bought bonds to the extent that was "far below" their purchasing ability. The names of these slackers, after they had been called by the executive committee and given a chance to "make good," will be posted on a bulletin board in the Oklahoma City Chamber of Commerce rooms and given to newspapers for publication. It was said to be this executive committee that was putting the "teeth" into the campaign. Bond slackers were reported to the committee by team captains and workers as rapidly as they were discovered. Ames or some other committee member then called the alleged slacker on the phone and asked for the reason for the person's refusal to buy or the "small amount" purchased. If a person refused to discuss the situation, he was invited "very, very firmly" to come to the Chamber of Commerce to explain in person. "In most instances he comes," noted a reporter. However, it was explained that the executive committee never went to a man's place of business to get an explanation.[1]

Equally worried about the situation in Oklahoma City at that time was the editor of a newspaper in that community. Worried that the purchase of Liberty bonds was not proceeding at a rate "which would indicate the loyalty of Oklahoma City," the editor declared, "So the time has come to find out who buys and who refuses to buy Liberty bonds. It is reported that small wage earners are subscribing at a more liberal rate than many who are viewed as rich people. Let us have a published list of bond buyers, together with the amounts of the individual subscriptions." He envisioned that the published list would contain the name, occupation, and amount of bonds bought – and by inference and omission, any absent names would denote financial slackers. Explained the editor; "Then we'll know who the slackers are, the financial slackers, the men who grip their money bags and expect others to go out and fight with sword and bayonet and also furnish the funds to feed and pay our armed forces." Then he went a little further when he advocated, "Let's have a published list of those who refuse to aid the great government in the crisis. Let's hold the rich slackers up to public scorn. This is no time to let the patriots fight the battles and permit the traitors to remain in a position of inactivity. For inactivity means hostility. Those who are not FOR the government are AGAINST the government." He continued, "And, after we get the published list of the financial slackers, let no one get the idea that we are through with them. Merely holding them up to public scorn doesn't finish the job. When the disloyal ones are known we're ready then to treat their cases as deserved. Let's have the names."[2]

One of the earliest men publicly named and shamed was an individual in Alta Vista, Kansas, who received that treatment in October 1917. It was reported that unless H. F. Dierking, cashier of the People's State Bank of Alta Vista Kansas, could offer an alibi, Liberty bond campaign managers would continue considering him a "bond slacker." A letter signed by Dierking, in his official capacity and on bank letterhead, was sent to Henry W. F. Wege of Eskridge, Kansas. It was in reply to a letter Wege had mailed to the bank in which he said he had decided to subscribe to Liberty bonds. However, Dierking, in his letter of reply, advised his customer against investing in the bonds and added that he, Dierking, had not purchased any because he did not want to tie up his money "in that kind of long time paper." In his letter, the cashier said the bonds were "OK." Still, Wege could put his money into term deposits of six months or 12 months in his bank that paid the same interest rate – four percent – and not be stuck with the Liberty bonds with a 30-year term. That letter, by unstated means, ended up in the hands of government officials.[3]

According to a news account, the Tulsa (OK) Army of Liberty was more than a pleading army begging people to buy Liberty bonds. It proposed to fight not simply to urge Americans to do their duty "but to hunt out those who are not Americans, or whose actions indicate they are not." [In their view, anyone who did not buy Liberty bonds, without an excuse acceptable to them, was not an American]. Posters distributed by the group bore such messages as; "Who's a slacker?" and "Where's Your Button?" [People who purchased a bond received a button that they wore on their clothing to "prove" their patriotism. It also had the benefit of limiting the amount of harassment a button-wearer was subjected to from bond solicitors roaming the streets, which they did]. Another poster slogan was, "There are two kinds: Americans and Enemies. Where's Your Button?" A button was considered necessary in Tulsa that last week in October as the Tulsa Army of Liberty was going all out in its efforts to sell bonds. N. R. Graham, director of Liberty Loan publicity in northern Oklahoma, admitted that week that the 2,000 Army of Liberty volunteer workers were obtaining and reporting the names of all persons who refused to purchase bonds. In Collinsville, Oklahoma, reportedly, a committee headed by J. D. Ward was publishing a list of the slackers in the newspapers each day. Said Graham; "Under government instructions we are obtaining the names of non-buyers of bonds and turning them over to the secret service division of the council of defense. I am not at liberty to say anything else along this line."[4]

An editor with an Indiana newspaper also favored publicity, declaring, "Relentless publicity and exposure must quickly follow efforts to spread disloyalty. In Kansas City, Mo., the patriots even believe that the names of persons who refuse to buy Liberty Bonds should be made public." As an example, he cited a news story from Kansas that declared John L. McLain of the Kansas City firm of Piggott and McLain as the first Kansas City businessman placed on the "official blacklist" in the Second Liberty Loan campaign. McLain refused to buy any bonds and was said to have been "insolent" to solicitors when they approached him and asked to purchase bonds. D. W. Ross, one of the solicitors, reported to committee chairman W. T. Kemper and said that McLain refused to buy a bond from himself and his partner E. C. Ellis and practically ordered the two canvassers from his store. Two other men financially able to take "a large bloc of bonds" were also placed on the blacklist. One was a downtown grocer [unnamed] to whom a special "odds and ends" committee of bond solicitors would give another chance. The other man was Dr. F. W. Froghling, a person of German descent who only "recently" had become a naturalized American citizen. After refusing bond solicitors, he told a special committee that he had bought a bond. He had purchased a single $50 bond, it was said, from a trust company, and he displayed his button when the committee called on him; "I want you fellows to leave me alone now," he told them. However, the committee felt that Dr. Froghling should have subscribed for a much greater amount of bonds.[5]

Kiowa County, Kansas, and its county seat Greensburg in particular were reported as unprepared to tolerate the slacker. Cited specifically was Ely Smyre, one of the richest men in the town and a man who had refused to give to the YMCA and also refused to let the public use his building on Main Street on Tribute Day – a day held in honor of the boys from the area who had been drafted into the military. Smyre refused to join the Red Cross campaign, and the citizens of Greensburg, showing their disapproval of the "slacker" Smyre, moved his building, which is frame, out in the street." That building was then decorated with signs that read, "Income $34.00 per day, local taxes practically 00, citizenship POOR." Another sign declared; "Red Cross Slacker," and another stated; "Donations to the Red Cross 00." The building was moved into the street on Saturday night, December 15, 1917, and the next day Kansas Governor

Arthur Capper made a public address on the same street in Greensburg, "and practically all of Kiowa county saw the monument of shame erected to Ely Smyre."[6]

Because some people in the Prescott, Arizona area refused to buy Liberty bonds and failed to offer any reason for doing so, it was suggested, declared a journalist, that a list of the names of those slackers be published in the newspapers of Yavapai County, "and the suggestion seems to be finding favor wherever proposed." It was not the intention of the loan committees to post as slackers any person who had a "really valid excuse" for not buying bonds "but merely to give a little publicity to the tight-wad personage who could buy bonds if he were so inclined, but refuses to do so through a lack of sympathy with the big movement Uncle Sam is promoting at present." Reportedly, a "committee of ladies" was making a systematic canvas of the city calling upon each residence and place of business to solicit purchases of bonds of the third issue. Those volunteer workers carried with them notebooks, and the name of each person contacted was listed in the notebooks, and a notation was added as to the type of reception received by the solicitors; "In cases where the person interviewed deliberately refuses to buy a bond, his name and address will be recorded, and some publicity more or less undesirable will in all probability come his way."[7]

The local Liberty Loan Committee at La Grande, Oregon, bought a full-page ad in the *La Grande Observer* to advise the people of that community and Union County that two of its citizens – Freeman Ladd and J. I. Kuhn – were slackers. The ad was signed by the committee and many "prominent" people of La Grande and Union County. The ad signers pledged never to transact business with the slackers or to allow them to enter other places of business or their homes. Said the editor of another Oregon newspaper; "This is a severe but effective way to treat 'those who are able but will not' support the government's financial needs."[8]

As of April 21, 1918, it was reported that every Oregon city was over the top with respect to their Liberty bond sales quota in the Third Liberty Loan drive. Nevertheless, Liberty Loan workers were "indignant on April 20 when a committee reported that Mrs. Sterett (perhaps Starratt), a teacher in A. T. Link's business college in Portland, had declined to buy a bond and had stated that she had never subscribed during earlier bond drives, nor had she given to the Red Cross. She said, further, that she would do nothing to aid the government in the war and would never subscribe to the bonds. Speaking on behalf of his private business college A. T. Link told the committee that they had not subscribed to the third drive "because of circumstances." However, said Link, the matter of Sterett's subscriptions was her affair and was not the business of himself or of his school. Link advised the committee that when he got ready to subscribe in his name or in the name of his business school, he would call at the bond headquarters and in the meantime bond solicitors should stay away from his institution. With respect to these "recalcitrant ones," the committee observed that; "They will be investigated further.[9]

Some ten days later, it was reported that; "Another liberty loan delinquent will enter the fold this morning" when Link, principal of Link's Business College, had agreed to appear at bond headquarters and subscribe to $250 worth of bonds in his name. To that point, he had not contributed to the loan, although he had been repeatedly solicited. One day earlier, he had been summoned to headquarters by Emery Olmstead, Liberty Loan chairman for Portland, Oregon, following an ultimatum that his students had reportedly issued. At that meeting, according to Olmstead, "He expressed a desire to participate in the loan, and dictated a statement disclaiming any knowledge of disloyalty in connection with his school." Later Link rescinded that statement telling Olmstead that he wished to revise it and present it one day later. It was asserted by loan workers "that the trend of instructive sentiment at his school was pacifist in type, and that advertising matter circulated to attract students was nothing less than cleverly worded hints at how to escape active military service."[10]

Their patience at an end, Liberty Loan officials, in early May 1918, gave up all attempts to persuade A. T. Link to buy a bond and "publicly branded him as a slacker of the most pronounced type." That action was taken after Link had rescinded his promise of the day before, made, both orally and in writing, to buy a bond and demanded the return of the pledge card which he had signed. Declared Emery Olmstead; "I am convinced, after speaking with Mr. Link for several hours and vainly endeavoring to persuade him to buy bonds, that he is an inveterate slacker and does not comprehend the significance of his actions." Olmstead added, "By his own indictment he had never bought a bond of any issue, and any person who is financially able to purchase a bond, as he admittedly is, by such action brands himself as a slacker." Portland Mayor George L. Baker, a member of the executive committee of the Third Liberty Loan, considered the advertisement by which Link sought to draw pupils to his school, holding out the offer of government employment, in contrast to the trenches and munitions factories, and Baker "sternly" criticized Link on that and other counts. On a Tuesday afternoon, Link called the Liberty bond headquarters and professed his willingness to buy a bond. At that time, he dictated and signed a statement outlining his attitude and declaring his loyalty. Shortly after issuing that statement and signing the bond pledge, Link asked that it be withdrawn as he desired to modify it. A couple of days later, Link again called headquarters and demanded the return of his pledge card. He informed workers at headquarters that he had changed his mind and would not buy a bond, asserting that he and his college had received unfavorable publicity. He was also criticized over the attitude of his employee at the business school, Miss Starrett, who was "an alleged pacifist..." Link told the committee, and the general public, that it was none of their business what views his instructors might hold. According to the news account, "Students of the business college have called at Liberty Temple [bond headquarters] and told officials of their determination to give up attendance. It is understood that the student body recently informed Link that his attitude did not meet with their approval, and that there would be a general walkout of all classes if he persisted in his decision not to buy a bond."[11]

Link's vacillations over whether or not to buy a bond ended on May 2 when he entered bond headquarters and bought a $100 bond. That came just after he had been publicly branded as a slacker. Students at the college had called a meeting for later that day at the bond headquarters. They were expected to ask Olmstead to review the entire affair, threatening to walk out of classes if they were not satisfied.[12]

Two days later, Link took out a wordy paid advertisement (identified as such) in the local newspapers. He offered a complete and abject apology for his behavior. Included in the text was a denial by Link of any disloyalty at any time by him or anyone on his staff. He also mentioned various contributions he had made to other organizations for the war effort. Link stated that Mrs. Link had two brothers then serving in the United States military, with one of them overseas fighting and the other still training in the United States. In summary, Link considered the whole affair to be a great injustice to himself.[13]

Alger Melton was the former chairman of the Oklahoma State Democratic Central Committee. In May 1918, he was chairman of the Grady County Council of Defense. Speaking in Chickasha, Oklahoma, after urging everyone to contribute to the best of their financial ability to the Third Liberty Loan, he authorized the statement that after "legitimate time" had been given to all to buy bonds in proportion to their resources, a list of names of those failing or refusing to do so would be made public. Melton, declared; "The man who buys a $50 or $100 bond when his financial condition and status is such that he should reasonably purchase $500 or $1,000 in bonds is just as much a slacker as is the man who is able to buy one bond and refuses to do so"[14]

An editorial in a Kansas newspaper noted that the practice of printing the names of Liberty bond slackers seems to meet with the approval of all but the said slackers. Reportedly the *Tyrone Observer* (OK) printed the "names and pedigrees" of some of them a week earlier, and the press of the county was "commending the paper for its stand and threatening to do likewise. And, after all, it is no more than they deserve.' This editor remarked that his newspaper had been asked repeatedly to print the names of slackers, "and if they do not come across one of these days we may yield to the request...nobody loves a slacker."[15]

An article published in an Olympia, Washington newspaper on May 10, 1918, was in the form of a letter signed by the Third Liberty Loan Committee, Thurston County, Washington. The piece began with the statement that there was an oversubscription in Thurston County for the Third Liberty Loan campaign – twice as much was raised in the county as was set as the allotment of $265,000 assigned and allocated to the county by the Washington State Liberty Loan Committee. Then the letter thanked all who had contributed before stating, "We, however, feel in duty bound to publicly state that there are men of means in Thurston county who failed to subscribe for Third Liberty Loan bonds, though amply able to do so" As far as this committee was concerned those who failed to subscribe could be divided into three classes; 1) people having pro-German sympathies 2) radical socialists 3) 'the extremely selfish, who desire higher interest rates." Among the people called to the attention of the committee and who failed to subscribe to the Third Liberty bond drive, although "amply" able to do so, were the following: "George Kemper, manager of the Washington Farm Loan Company; J. B. Sudman, proprietor of a second-hand store at 214 West Fourth Street; Adam Johnson, proprietor of the Washington Store, 427 Main Street; A. Mosher, proprietor of the Capital Poultry Company, 212 West Fourth Street; H. E. Cunningham, proprietor of a grocery store, 1015 Tenth Street; J. H. Blass, oysterman; A. Benson, proprietor of a grocery store, 209 West Fourth Street; James Compton, employee of the Buchanan Lumber company."[16]

One week later, an editorial appeared in the above newspaper that commented on the names that had been published. Said the editor; "Undoubtedly there are others besides those whose names were published by the Liberty Loan committee last week, who should have been listed among them, persons of whom the committee did not know or persons who bought a fifty or a hundred dollar bond just to 'get in under the wire,' when their financial circumstances warranted a purchase of several hundred dollars."[17]

How Garfield County Washington treated its bond and Red Cross slackers was described in a newspaper published at Pomeroy Washington and one from Lynden Washington, with each stating it; "takes a great deal of pleasure in reprinting the account because of the suggestion given in it of how to handle unpatriotic citizens of this unpleasant type." According to the Pomeroy paper, "The Patriotic League of Colfax (WA) publishes A. M. and B. N. Butcher as liberty bond slackers" and sends a letter to Pomeroy containing the following paragraph. "The patriotic league has published these men here as slackers and has asked all people here to ostracize them socially, commercially and every other way. We give this information as patriotic citizens and may we ask the people of Pomeroy to likewise treat them as social outcasts." The matter was put before a meeting of the Pomeroy Commercial Club, and the following resolution was passed by the club. "Whereas: A. M. Butcher and B. N. Butcher of Wordesville P.O., Garfield County, Washington, each have insolently refused to purchase Liberty bonds, or Thrift stamps, notwithstanding they are amply able to do so: Therefore, Be it resolved, that it is the sense of Pomeroy Commercial Club, that its members and all patriotic citizens refrain from all association commercially, socially or otherwise with the said A. M. Butcher and B. N. Butcher and all other persons financially able, who have refused to purchase Liberty Bonds or Thrift Stamps, or to contribute to the Red Cross." And that; "It is further resolved that a committee be appointed to notify all business men of Pomeroy, Starbuck, Colfax and Lewiston and all county stores of this action and urge them to refrain from any dealings or associations with all such 'Slackers!'"[18]

It was reported in July 1918 that Tennessee's thrift stamp "slacker list" that "may cause a mild social furor upon publication" was rapidly being compiled, and Hamilton County's section of that list "will have a personnel which is surprising." It was said to be the plan of the War Savings Stamps committee to publish the list of names in each county of "men in that section whose means are known to be ample, but who have failed to purchase thrift stamps. Those whose purchases are ludicrously small will also be added." Richard Hardy, vice-director, and Nora A. Parker, secretary of the Tennessee state committee, were to attend a meeting in Nashville where representatives of 18 counties which failed to meet their quota in bond sales would discuss plans to meet their quotas; "These counties are not to be allowed to fall short and a second drive of some sort will be desired to complete the quotas." T. R. Preston, state director of the committee, commented on the situation by saying that it was beyond his understanding how people could refuse to respond to "these patriotic plans for financing the war."[19]

A week later, a follow-up report from Tennessee stated the prospects of publishing a thrift stamp slacker list was having a "remarkable effect" all over the state, according to T. R. Preston. He said bond committee headquarters were being "deluged" with letters in explanation, and subscriptions were fast filling the quotas so that the state quota was expected to be reached within the next 30 to 60 days. Said Preston; "As the quotas were established upon a basis of population in the face of the large negro population of the south, a large percentage of which could not be depended upon for their pro rata, an exceptional burden has fallen upon the shoulders of the more financially able to subscribe."[20]

Waterloo, Iowa, had a Liberty Loan system that provided for the publication of names of bond slackers. Allotments as to how much people should spend on bonds were made in Marshalltown, Iowa. Committees had been sitting as "boards of equalization" at the YMCA for five days as 400 citizens came forward to complain about the bond quota assigned to them. Those who refused to meet their final allotment were brought before the judge advocate's court or the military court of the war service league. According to a journalist, "If they fail to come across then their names are published in the newspapers as slackers and are forwarded to Washington on yellow cards." In Marshalltown, "We have the committee on loyalty of the council of defense and the yellow card which the Treasury department at Washington furnishes but we have not resorted to publishing the names of bond slackers. Here is an idea"[21]

Faithful to their promises, officials of the Portland Oregon Liberty Loan committee made public, on September 30, 1918, the names of three men whom they charged "with failure to meet the obligations of the fourth liberty loan. The committee declares that additions will be made to the list, if special solicitors now at work fail to bring in favorable reports on other cases." Charged by the committee with "failure to properly support the fourth loan" were

John Clark of the Clark Saddlery Company, William Isensee of 206 North 24th Street, and C. Welk of 4121 42nd Street, Southwest. Wearied by "constant rebuffs on the part of citizens who have declined to buy bonds, or who have not subscribed in amounts considered fitting to their resources" committee officials held a meeting and decided to give the public the names of alleged shirkers and slackers. As far as the committee was concerned, a slacker was defined as a person or firm who could buy bonds but did not. A shirker was a person or firm who bought "a grossly inadequate amount, obviously much less than he or she should buy." John Clark subscribed for $500 worth of bonds, yet, the committee declared he was worth over $200,000 and had government contracts to a value of $250,000. C. Welk was described as a slacker who "does not believe in buying bonds. His case is now in the hands of the Department of Justice." William Isensee was a slacker who refused to buy any bonds and had also been reported to the federal Department of Justice "under the provisions of the espionage act. This man was extremely troublesome in the third liberty loan campaign, and was brought before the police department and the Department of Justice at that time, on similar charges."[22]

Portland's release of the above names coincided with the opening of that city's campaign for the Fourth Liberty Loan drive. The Portland Liberty Loan Committee was headed by Guy W. Talbot and Emery Olmstead, chairman. Journalist Ben Hur Lampman noted that Portland's campaign would open "with a decisive attack upon incomes and bank accounts that seem to warrant larger subscriptions than those already recorded." A resolution adopted by the Portland Liberty Loan Committee declared; "Whereas from the canvass made to this date by the liberty loan organization for subscriptions to the fourth liberty loan, it conclusively appears that there is a very substantial number of men in professional and business vocations in good circumstances and who enjoy substantial incomes, but who have not subscribed in proportion to their resources, but are permitting the more prominent capitalists and the laboring men to assume the burden at hand; now, therefore, be it Resolved that each business and profession be classified and that a committee of three be appointed in each class, who will rate each member thereof; that with each rating will be listed the amount subscribed by the man rated; that, thereupon, said rated member be notified of his rating and appear and show cause why he should not subscribe to the amount of his rating; that, if no good cause be shown why he should not so subscribe, that his name, rating and amount subscribed be published in the daily press; and, to the end that no injustice may be done, be it further Resolved, that investigation be made of available Government and private records that the liberty loan committee may ascertain the income and resources of the person so rated as aforesaid." Illustrative was the "authentic" story of a wealthy contractor who bought a $50 bond. When his pledge was checked at headquarters, evidence was produced to show that he was amply able to subscribe to a larger amount and that his business was thriving. Because of that check at headquarters, "A special solicitor visited him and met his rebuffs with absolute refusal to leave until the matter had been thrashed out. The controversy closed with a liberty loan subscription of $5000."[23]

An editor with a different Oregon newspaper mentioned Portland's supposed attention to the wealthy residents and the idea of publicizing their names as slackers, if necessary. Then the editor noted, concerning his county; "In Umatilla County, all the newspapers are under pledge to provide such publicity when requested by the Umatilla County Patriotic Service League."[24]

Edward Cookingham was chairman of the executive committee for the Oregon Liberty Loan campaign, and John L. Etheridge was the state director of that organization. On a day in October 1918, they reported that S. L. Scroggin, president of the First National

Bank of Sheridan, Oregon, had been classed as a bond slacker. No details were given, but a reporter observed that; "In making his name public they said they had turned to publicity as a fully justified step toward his reform."[25]

According to local Liberty Loan chairman August Gronwoldt, the work of combing the town of Redding, California, for slackers was progressing. He urged all who knew of shirkers to report them to the authorities. Whenever a man had bought less than he should, a special committee would investigate the circumstances before "the man is publicly posted as a slacker and his name sent to the State Council of Defense." He assured people that every man who failed to subscribe "or puts over any camouflage patriotism by subscribing less than he can afford will be publicly posted as a slacker and turned over to the authorities."[26]

An article on page 1 of an Oregon newspaper did so in the form of an open letter "To the public" from the Central Loyalty Committee, Umatilla County Patriotic Service League. That piece brought to the public's attention the name of Higby Harris of Milton [now Milton-Freewater], Oregon, as "one who has consistently and flagrantly failed in the support of his government at war. It believes that the word 'slacker' was coined for just such men as he." Harris had lived in Umatilla County for many years and had grown wealthy there. He was, reportedly, generally credited with being the richest man in the east end of the county and was paying taxes under his name on real property assessed at $75,000 and personal property assessed at $10,000. A "very conservative" estimate of his wealth was $175,000. Harris did not subscribe to the First Liberty loan nor the Second Liberty loan. During the Third Liberty loan, when an organization for rounding up delinquents was created, he subscribed for $2,500. That was the amount of his subscription, also for the Fourth Liberty Loan. However, "He refused to subscribe for his rating of $4,000." He was notified to appear before the committee named above and make excuses. Still, he simply ignored the notice to appear. Thus, the committee decided to expose him publicly. In the Second Red Cross War Fund campaign, Harris refused to contribute so much as $1, and the committee had no record of his having donated to any war fund; "On the other hand we have received innumerable reports to the effect that he has thousands of dollars on deposit and has openly stated that he intends holding his money until after the war so that he will be in a position to buy land when values shrink." The committee added that it "believes that there is no one man in the county whose example has been the cause of so much dissatisfaction. We hope there are few citizens in America who have given such niggardly support and who have manifested a spirit of such grudging patriotism." The article then listed John H. Peters, Frank Hilbert, and L. C. Rothrock, all of whom had been summoned to hearings before the committee. Then it added that Peters had that very day agreed to subscribe to his "full quota." At the same time, Hilbert authorized his subscription to be increased to $4,000, which was the amount of his quota. Rothrock was out of town when summoned and thus was granted more time.[27]

Two days later, it was reported that a phone call from Milton indicated that Higby Harris had subscribed to his full quota of Liberty bonds, that is, $4,000. That phone call was from a bank clerk in a Milton bank to the Patriotic Services League. That caused the League to announce that its strategy of publicizing the names of slackers was "bearing fruit." By this date, everyone whose names had been publicized subscribed to their full quotas, except for Rothrock, who remained out of the country. And, the League boasted, "A large number of others who have been hanging back in meeting their ratings are also coming forward to avoid the ignominy of being branded slackers."[28]

Publication of the names of all persons who had subscribed for bonds of the Fourth Liberty Loan drive in Phoenix would begin in the middle of October 1918, according to a news account. It was slated to continue until all the names had been published, and the listings would be done by the denomination of the bond. That is, one day, the paper would print the names of all people who had purchased a $50 bond; the next day, the list would be of all those who had bought a $100 bond, and so on. And, said the report, "Meanwhile, compilation of the list of heads of families in this county who have not subscribed to bonds of the first, second, third or fourth loans is going on with a view to an early publication of the names of those who for one reason or another have not been recorded as subscribing to any of the Liberty loans."[29]

In Michigan, the Gratiot County War Board came out strongly against the Liberty Loan slacker, saying, "such men will find small comfort from their neighbors once the campaign is over, as the board has determined on publishing the names of the slackers in the newspapers of the county." Also, stated a reporter, "There is no question but what the newspapers of the county will gladly aid the war board in this step. They feel that Gratiot has no room for slackers, and will back any good move in this direction."[30]

G. E. M. Pratt, president and treasurer of the Sunset Motor Company, which was the local agency in Seattle, Washington, for the Cadillac and Hupmobile automobiles, was, on October 10, 1918, branded a Liberty Bond slacker by the executive committee of the local Liberty Loan committee, of which C. S. Wills was the chairman. At the same time, Gamma Poncin, president of the Yesler estate, one of the wealthiest realty firms in Seattle, was also branded a bond slacker by the same group. Said a statement issued by that executive committee; "Committees have repeatedly called upon Poncin and he has kept them waiting in the ante-room and then treated them discourteously and indifferently. He stated he would buy $5,000 of bonds, and that was the best he could do, and; after repeated calls finally said he would purchase $15,000, but upon this basis Seattle will never raise its quota as he is well able to purchase the amount of his rating." According to the committee Judge Burke and several other "prominent" citizens called on Pratt. He told them he had put $23,000 in the Red Cross barrels and could not buy as many bonds as was expected from him. When questioned, Pratt explained he meant two or three thousand. When Burke told him there was no record of such a donation to the Red Cross in Seattle, Pratt explained further that he put that amount of money in the Red Cross barrels in Chicago.[31]

In explaining the publication of the above two names, King County Liberty Loan chairman C. S. Wills observed that he had promised the public would be allowed to know who the bond slackers were in King County, thus the publication of the two names. Wills noted that repeated opportunities were given to those men to do their share, and after they had repeatedly refused to "see the light," it was decided to let the public know their attitudes. Said a journalist; "Pitiless publicity will be used to acquaint Seattle with wealthy men who refuse to do their part."[32]

Complaints about a lagging sale of bonds during the Fourth Liberty Loan drive were reported from Arizona, with grumblings from Maricopa County that the area had not much more than half of the subscribers for the Fourth drive, as compared to the Third Liberty Loan campaign. H. G. Saylor, a well-to-do farmer from the Mesa district, who lived near Tempe, Arizona, was the only bond slacker reported by the workers of the Mesa committee as never having subscribed to a Liberty bond of any issue. Saylor was "brought" into bond headquarters and allowed to explain. He told his questioners that he worshiped a god who did not believe in war, so he did not want to buy any bonds. When asked if he did not believe in protecting his home and family, he maintained that his god would look after him. Saylor said he had donated $25 to the Red Cross since the war had begun but had not supported the war in any other way. While Saylor maintained his refusal at the end of the session with the committee, that group insisted that the investigation of Saylor had "only begun."[33]

A day later, Saylor had a change of heart because it was reported that he sent in his check for a $500 bond. Observed a reporter; "It is generally recognized among those who have known Mr. Saylor for a long time that this was a case of unreasonable religious conceptions far more than any sympathy for Germany." It was said to be a matter of relief to those "who really do not wish for him the unpleasant results sure to follow any slackerism, that the matter has been adjusted..."[34]

A black newspaper in Phoenix, Arizona, observed that the Colored Liberty Loan committee announced that on October 19, 1918, the names of all "colored citizens" in Phoenix who had bought bonds of the Fourth Liberty Loan issue would appear in the *Phoenix Tribune* under the heading "Honor Roll of Colored Citizens who have bought bonds of the Fourth Liberty Loan." Those who had not bought bonds would also have their names published – under the caption "Slackers." However, a search of that weekly paper for that date and the rest of 1918 revealed that no such lists were ever published.[35]

Seattle returned to list more names of slackers a week after publicly naming slackers Pratt and Poncin. This time the local Liberty Loan committee pointed the finger at Henry Landes and W. L. Gwinn. Landes was the head of a land company the committee had rated as able to buy from $10,000 to $15,000 worth of bonds. He had only subscribed, though, for $400 worth. Gwinn headed Gwinn Investment Company. He was rated as able to buy from $5,000 to $10,000 but had bought only $750 worth of bonds. And it was reported that; "Gwinn has been putting up a lot of small houses recently which he has sold at fancy profits. He told Chairman Wills

that he had $20,000 in the banks. He has two boys at the front –
and so he takes the attitude he has done his share." The committee
also branded the corporation Armour & Company as "unfair" to
Seattle because it even sent the subscriptions of local employees,
amounting to $10,850, to Chicago, to be registered as purchases
made in Chicago thus making it more difficult for Seattle to reach its
city and county quotas. It was also noted that Armour & Company
and other outside corporations doing business in Seattle had bank
balances in that city. That increased the total deposits in Seattle
banks. The city's quota for the Liberty Loan campaign was partly
based on that figure of total bank deposits: "If these corporations
refuse to contribute their share in Seattle, they impose a greater
hardship on the rest of the people."[36]

There was an appeal near the end of the Fourth Liberty Loan
campaign from the Fairmont West Virginia Liberty Loan
organization urging people not to be bond slackers. By their
definition, "A bond slacker is not merely the man or woman who
buys no bonds, but also the one who buys only to the extent of his
convenience and is not willing to make any real sacrifice" Noted also
was that it had been repeatedly suggested that the names of the bond
slackers be published as they would then be held up to the contempt
of the community, as was deserved. But, perhaps publication was
unnecessary, "Such publication of names, however, is entirely
unnecessary, as the mouth-to-mouth publicity in such cases is quite
sufficient. The time has come when a man has a right to discuss his
neighbor's affairs, as they are his own as well, since no man can live
unto himself. Since Mr. Jones' son is fighting for the liberty enjoyed
by Mr. Smith, the latter should not resent it if Mr. Jones insists that
he do his part in aiding the government to equip and support his
son." The newspaper asserted, "Any one who does not buy bonds
to the very limit of his or her ability in order that our boys 'over
there' may be well equipped for defense and offense, is permitting

some brave young American to sacrifice all the rosy-hued ambitions of youth; to suffer all the hardships of war with its burning thirst' its stifling gas and excruciating pain; to shed his blood on a foreign soil with no loved hand to minister, no soft touch to soothe – and for what? For a craven and an ingrate who holds his dollar so close to his eye that it excludes from his vision all the larger, higher nobler things that go to make up real life."[37]

As they did their work, the members of the local Liberty Loan Committee in La Habra, California, found only one slacker and because an "aroused" public opinion "demanded" to know who the slackers were. In following the instruction of the California Council of Defense, they publicly named him. During that Fourth loan drive and on all three previous drives, no one had ever been able to induce Fred R. Aldrich to purchase a bond. However, the earlier statement was contradicted when it was stated that he had purchased one $50 bond in the Third Liberty Loan drive. During the Fourth drive, Aldrich reportedly promised one of the bond solicitors that he would purchase bonds on the 15th of October. He said he expected to have some money to buy bonds by that date. On the 15th, the solicitor returned, and Aldrich told him he had kept his word and bought a bond. When the solicitor asked where he had purchased it, Aldrich replied, "That is easy enough to find out, the records will show." However, the committee could locate no such purchase record after examining all available records. Aldrich owned 50 acres of land at La Habra, assessed at $15,000, improvements assessed at $1,250, and owned personal property valued at $1,120. That meant his property was worth at least $50,000. As far as the committee was concerned, such a property value meant Aldrich should have subscribed to at least several thousand dollars worth of bonds instead of a single $50 purchase.[38]

An ad that took up about two-thirds of a page in the newspaper was placed by the Fourth Liberty Loan committee of Spokane, Washington. It began by explaining Spokane was short of reaching its Liberty bond quota and, "This money must be raised. Spokane must not fail in its duty to the country." That ad was said to be the first in a series to follow in which stories of slackers would be laid before the public. Then example number one was given and named. Sylvester Heath of 613 Mission Avenue was a 35-year-old Spokane resident. Heath stated he had subscribed for $1,100 worth of bonds in the Fourth drive. However, it was reported, "The quota set by the rating committee as the amount Mr. Heath should subscribe is $25,000." Heath was estimated to be worth several hundred thousand dollars, invested in various local properties and securities of various kinds. "The mutual growth of the city and the energy of Mr. Heath's fellow citizens made him a wealthy man," declared the ad, but Heath refused to subscribe for more than $1,100.[39]

Frank Peterson was a rancher who lived southeast of Mesa, Arizona. On October 14, 1918, Ed Pattee, who was in charge of the slacker work for the Maricopa County Liberty Loan committee, spent considerable time with several of his colleagues trying to persuade Peterson "as to his duty" to buy bonds. It was remarked that this case had the same "unfortunate aspect" to it that had come up in other cases, that is, "a religious objection to subscribing." Peterson owned 120 acres of good land and was considered a hard-working and respected community member. One night, a few days earlier, a committee argued with him for two hours but to no avail as he continued to insist he could not justify himself in subscribing. He claimed to be a Red Cross contributor. Peterson was handed the "official book on German atrocities," and he promised to read it. Committee chairman Loftus, in giving him the book to read, "urged him to try and get straight on the matter."[40]

Pressure was applied again as three men, including Peterson, were brought up before the committee on October 16. All stated they were conscientious objectors to the idea of bond purchases. The other two were G. F. Turner, a farmer two miles from Tempe, Arizona, and Dr. Louis Dysart of Phoenix. In all three cases, the men continued to refuse to purchase bonds. It was reported at that time that the merchants of Tempe had refused to buy from or sell to Turner because of the attitude he had assumed and that an effigy of Peterson had been placed on the main street of Mesa.[41]

A day or so after the effigy of Peterson was placed on public display, bearing the legend that he was a Liberty Loan slacker, it was reported that he had left his ranch without telling any of his friends where he was going or even saying goodbye to them. He had been preparing to leave when the local committee got wind of the idea and told him it would not be wise for him to go, but he left anyway. Peterson was also said to bear the "unenviable reputation" of leaving Texas just in time to escape from a loan drive in that area. When his departure from Mesa was made known, a picture was taken from the effigy bearing his name and sent to his former hometown in Texas, where he was said to still have banking interests.[42]

A day later, a newspaper account declared that; "The Maricopa County liberty loan committee is running the pocketbook slackers to earth and doing it with a vengeance. Already coats of yellow paint have been administered to men who have refused to buy bonds. Doctors, merchants, and farmers have been up before the committee to explain the lack of purchases. Some of these have come through while others have ignored all appeals." Chairman of the committee, J. N. Gaines, sent out a telegram, in the wake of his apparent disappearance from Mesa, to neighboring communities; Delay Frank Peterson, yellow slacker and wealthy man, aged 45; five feet eight inches tall, weight about 220 pounds and driving a Studebaker, with Texas license number 215539. Notify patriotic garages not to sell gasoline. Stop his supply there and elsewhere. Destination Sour Lake, Tex." That wire was signed by Edward Pattee, vice-chairman of the Liberty Loan Committee.[43]

According to loan campaign officials, the names of 19 "prominent" citizens who either had not subscribed to the Liberty Loan or had not subscribed as fully as their financial circumstances warranted were to be published in local morning and afternoon papers on October 18, 1918. Lists of other alleged loan slackers were to be published daily until all the names in possession of loan campaign officials were made public.[44]

The Lee County Illinois Fourth Liberty Loan committee officially closed for business in mid-October 1918 when the Fourth drive officially ended. Of the 8,500 people listed for subscriptions but not having signed up just two weeks earlier, only eight failed to "take their allotment." The committee had erected a large slacker board on the public square in Dixon, Illinois, and the eight names were placed on the board. According to a journalist, "A great crowd witnessed the proceedings. Lee county's allotment was subscribed the first day, but the committee insisted that all delinquents should come up to their quota notwithstanding."[45]

A dispatch from Douglas, Arizona, stated that if Fred Colter became governor of Arizona and an additional judge was created for Cochise County, Arizona, S. W. White of Douglas would get the job. White, it was observed, was cited at the head of the Liberty Loan committee's list of Douglas bond slackers by two of the local newspapers. He subscribed to bonds but then refused to pay for them. The list was published in the local newspapers in alphabetical order except for White's name, which was placed at the head, "possibly because he is the chief slacker." That problem never arose as Colter did not become the Arizona governor.[46]

A statement issued on October 24, 1918, in South Bend, Indiana, by an official with the loan committee in that area was presented as a reiteration of "my former warnings." That statement came from the Board of Review, "which passes finally on the patriotism of those who have failed to do their full duty in the purchase of Liberty bonds." Said the statement, "Unless those citizens of South Bend and St. Joseph county who have so far failed to do their full share in the purchase of fourth Liberty loan bonds appear before the board of review at its meeting...Sat. Afternoon [26th] and either show good cause for not purchasing their full quota of bonds or buy their full quota then, their names will be published." There were reported to be at least 30 people who had not bought their total share and failed to give any satisfactory reason for not doing so. Unless those 30 appeared and gave valid reasons, their names would be published. Since the campaign for bond sales in the Fourth Liberty Loan in St. Joseph County officially closed, on October 19, over 100 people who failed to meet their quota had been called before the Board of Review. At least 70 of them made up their full quota or gave satisfactory reasons for not doing so. It was also reported that the Liberty Loan committee planned to send copies of the published list of those who failed to buy their full quota of bonds "to the soldiers from the county who are either in training camps in this country or who are in the trenches overseas."[47]

The name of Dr. C. W. Evans, described as a "prominent and wealthy physician" of Modesto, California, was published by the area Council of Defense for failure to buy Liberty bonds. The organization stated Evans was asked to subscribe to $5,000 worth of bonds as the Council felt that was the least amount he should purchase because of the fact he had not subscribed to any bonds of the First or Second issues and only $2,000 bought during the Third issue drive. Evans offered to take $2,000 during the Fourth drive, but that offer was refused by officials. A committee then visited Evans, but he again refused to take more than $2,000 worth. Evans argued he had been one of the examining physicians [for inductees] and that his services were worth $100 a day, but he had charged nothing for such work and thus considered that as part of his patriotic duty. As a counterargument, the committee pointed out to Evans that other physicians were doing the same thing, but none used that as an excuse for not buying bonds. On the following day, Evans mailed in a check for $3,000 to the committee, but it was returned to him with a plea that he buy $5,000 worth of bonds. This he refused to do, demanding, instead, that his offer of $3,000 be accepted. Evans was again asked to meet with the committee, but he failed to appear at the specified time, and the committee agreed that his name was to be published as a slacker. Dr. Evans was described as one of the wealthiest men in Stanislaus County. A reporter remarked, "Many local people are provoked at the council for not demanding $25,000 instead of five thousand. It is said that many patients are being moved from the Evans sanitarium on account of the recent development."[48]

James Vickery, described as a Leading non-partisan" worker of Latah County, Idaho, was called before the Latah County Council of Defense at Moscow, Idaho, to explain his failure to subscribe to his share of the Fourth Liberty Loan campaign. It was stated that; "He is very abusive to members of the committee and denied their right to ask him to buy liberty bonds." Vickery admitted having sold a farm for $12,000 that week but said he should not be required to buy bonds with any of that money. Vickery threatened to get even with the members of the county council after the war was over. Remarked a journalist, "The county council has had many alleged bond slackers before it, but Mr. Vickery proved the hardest customer they have had to handle. He is thoroughly socialistic. He was ordered to buy $500 of war savings stamps but, so far as known, has not complied with the order."[49]

An item, in the form of an open letter signed by R. B. Millard, chairman of the Morrison County Minnesota Fourth Liberty Loan campaign, appeared in the local newspapers. It declared, "Although our county has gone over the top, those who have not taken their allotment of bonds are being asked to do so...The man who can and will not do his fair share in these times should have his rights as an American citizen taken from him." In cases of foreigners living here and who can buy bonds "and yet do not wish to do anything to show they are loyal should have their property taken from them and forced to return to their home country. It was the intention of the Central Committee to publish the names in the near future of all Liberty loan slackers in Morrison County."[50]

An editorial in an Iowa newspaper cited the activity that had transpired in Gladbrook, Iowa, part of Tama County, with respect to the area's YMCA allotments meted out to its residents. That is, the amount of money each resident should give to the YMCA for its war work. It was noted that Tama County had oversubscribed the quota allotted to the area, which meant organization and hard work; "All the people were assessed, each according to his financial ability, as viewed by the committee...The assessments ran from $1 to $25, except that the banks were asked for $50 and $30. There were few of the $25 class. Many were asked to give $15, or lesser amounts." The local newspaper in the Gladbrook area printed the entire list of allotments, giving in adjoining columns the amount each citizen was assessed and the amount they paid; "In nearly all cases payment of the amount asked was made...There were few slackers who would pay nothing and a few who would give only a fraction of the sum requested." Reportedly, 95 percent of the residents paid the amount they had been assessed; "Slackers are marked by stars and those stars are apt to make the fellows see stars whose names appear in front of them. The list is remarkable because of its novelty, and because of the practical, sensible idea involved." One example given was that of a "rich" farmer who was assessed $25 but only paid $2; "The financial slackers must be exposed just as the drafted slackers are dealt with...The rich men who have prospered under its liberal laws and unequaled opportunities must not dodge their duties longer. If they will not pay their share of the cost of this war willingly they must be made to pay it unwillingly." The newspaper editor discussed the issue and appreciated the method; "The Gladbrook way is a good way to loosen them. Other Tama county localities could use it with profit and satisfaction in future drives for war needs."[51]

Lady Lucy Duff Gordon worked out of New York City and designed gowns for Lucille Limited. She received $365 a week for her services and permitted her name to be signed to articles in the Hearst publications. She did not write those articles but received $100 weekly for them. While under examination in supplemental proceedings in court in New York City, completely unrelated to war bonds, she stated that she had not bought any Liberty bonds, although it was her "uncertain recollection" that her maid bought a $50 bond for her. The examination of Gordon was to determine what assets she had to satisfy a judgment against her in favor of Muriel Ridley for breach of contract. When she was asked in court if she had bought any Liberty bonds, she replied, "No; why should I? This country is nothing to me. I have had nothing but trouble here. This is an awful country."[52]

Chapter 7. Force and Coercion.

The most extreme reaction to those who refused to buy any liberty bonds, or were deemed by outside judgments to have not purchased as many as they should have, was the use of coercion and physical force of one kind or another. Hapless victims were subjected to being painted with yellow paint, being tarred and feathered, losing their jobs, being paraded about their communities in a manner designed to humiliate, and being physically beaten up. Mainly such events were conducted "unofficially," but on occasion, the legal system or community officials were actively involved. The many editorial comments cited earlier that, in a vague or not-so-vague manner, advocated that such drastic measures be applied to the bond slackers perhaps had a hand in instigating and legitimizing such events. Only a few examples of the use of force or coercion made it into the public record in 1917. A teamster and his son appeared before Police Judge Vaughan in Akron, Ohio, in June 1917 on charges of "special intoxication." The event stemmed from family troubles, and Vaughan concluded that the public interest would not be injured if no fine was meted out to the two men. However, Vaughan noted that the United States was at war and that Liberty bonds were being sold to finance the war and declared, "It is a patriotic act to buy a bond. I suggest that you buy one." The unnamed teamster saw the logic of the "suggestion." He purchased three $100 bonds, one for himself, one for his son, and one for his wife.[1]

That same month, adopting what a reporter called a "unique and effective" method, the community of Drumright, Oklahoma, collected $1,501 in one day of a Red Cross drive then underway across the nation. Under the leadership of City Clerk A. J. Fogaley, acting as a volunteer "policeman," officials rounded up those defined as Red Cross slackers. He ordered them to the city hall where a "kangaroo court" was held and fines assessed according to the estimated ability of those forced to contribute. Those "fines" ranged from $1 to $25. The judges, prosecuting attorneys, and court bailiffs involved were local Red Cross workers described as "local society leaders." That $1,501 was over and above the nearly $1,000 raised by the Drumright local auxiliary of the Red Cross during the previous month.[2]

Supposedly "patriotic indignation" at the refusal of the owner of the only assembly hall in Aspinwall, Iowa, a village near Manilla, Iowa, to permit the use of his place by Liberty Loan campaigners stirred more than 75 citizens of Manilla to such a state of resentment that they descended upon the small community of Aspinwall, closed all its stores, obtained the arrest of the uncooperative hall owner, John Brus, and obtained subscriptions for almost the entire quota of the township's bond allotment. The names of many citizens of the town, which was a German settlement, who did not buy a bond were given to the federal authorities for investigation, and the Iowa Council of Defense ordered the resignation of the town marshal. It all started, allegedly, when it was reported in Manilla that residents of Aspinwall were given to scornful laughter when approached by Liberty bond salesmen, and though Manilla itself was mainly populated by Germans, the mayor in that city organized, noted a journalist; "a flying squadron of boosters and business men, put them in fifteen automobiles and set out to see that Liberty Bond Day was celebrated in Aspinwall in a substantial way." A United States deputy marshal was in the squadron, and when Brus reiterated his refusal to open his hall for a Liberty loan meeting, he placed Brus under arrest. Mrs. Brus turned over the keys to the hall, and the meeting for the bond drive was held; "every able-bodied resident was forced to attend. Not a business house remained open, and subscriptions suddenly began to roll in." Brus was released relatively quickly, but the next day he could be found "pleading" with his German friends to buy bonds. When he was released, pending good behavior, he was told that if Iowa Township, where he resided, bought $25,000 worth of bonds, citizens would "attempt" to have the charges against him dropped. Immediately Brus purchased a $500 bond for himself and quickly began the selling campaign among his friends and acquaintances. Another result was that the American Stars and Stripes flag could be seen flying over business establishments and private homes in Aspinwall "for the first time in the memory of the oldest inhabitant."[3]

The action against Brus followed his refusal on Tuesday, Oct 23, 1917, to let the Liberty Loan people use his hall; his hall was the only one in town. Brus was arrested near midnight on the 23rd by State Marshal H. Yackey and taken to Council Bluffs, Iowa, where he was incarcerated on a charge of obstructing the Liberty Loan drive in Crawford County. He had agreed to rent the auditorium to Mayor Roscoe Saunders of Manilla and other "patriotic" citizens who would have held the Liberty loan meeting on the evening of the 23rd. However, when the people showed up, the hall was dark, and Brus was nowhere in sight. Liberty bond "patriots" stood around for half an hour while some Aspinwall businessmen, it was reported, "jeered and hooted at them. After waiting for a time, the visitors then gave up, jumped back into their cars, and left town without holding their meeting. Mayor Saunders called Iowa Governor William L. Harding at 10 PM. After explaining the situation to Harding, Saunders was authorized to arrest Brus. During the trip to the Council Bluffs lockup Brus, it was said, "made a confession according to the authorities in which he admitted there had been a preconceived move on the part of the Aspinwall 'kaiser-lovers' to prevent the liberty loan meeting." Brus implicated at least half a dozen Germans in Aspinwall with being involved in the plot. On the afternoon of October 23, Mayor Saunders of Manilla and other "patriots" planned to visit every German home in Aspinwall to "seize every picture of the kaiser and every German flag, and march the pro-Germans to the town hall, where a rousing liberty bond meeting is to be held." Brus was described as a "wealthy resident" of the area. Besides his auditorium, he operated a pool room and soft drink parlor in front of the auditorium. During Saunders' inquiry into events, it was reported that Brus had been heard to declare, "I am going to be out of town Tuesday night and then they can't hold the meeting." He also reportedly asserted that; "Those people had better stay in Manilla and mind their own business." Liberty bond boosters had experienced difficulties with other people in the Aspinwall area besides Brus. Charles Schutt, a wealthy German farmer who owned a 900-acre farm in the area, had refused to buy bonds or subscribe to the Red Cross. According to a journalist, he was taken into a back room of the Manilla bank on Tuesday, October 23, "and given a straight-from-the-shoulder talk, and finally bought $1,000 worth" of the bonds. Another wealthy German farmer, Johannes Peterson, had agreed to buy bonds, but when his wife heard about it, she stopped the proposed purchase. Two Manilla bankers, accompanied by Saunders, visited the Peterson farm on the afternoon of October 23, but no one responded to their knocks. Nevertheless, the delegation entered the house anyway and confronted Mrs. Peterson. When she reiterated the family would not buy bonds, she received a lecture on patriotism for half an hour and finally said her husband could buy a single $50 bond [the smallest denomination that could be purchased]. That caused the delegation to unleash "a verbal fusillade," and when it ended, Mrs. Peterson instructed her husband to buy $500 worth of bonds. He did.[4]

F. J. Schwalen was the president and cashier of the Triumph State Bank located in Triumph, Minnesota. Late in October 1917, he was arrested in Triumph by Sheriff Carver and charged with interference with the sale of Liberty Loan bonds. F. Wade. Chairman of the Liberty Loan Committee for Martin County explained that he asked Schwalen what action he intended to take to sell the bonds and was met with the following reply, "I can tell you damned quick what my bank is going to do. It isn't going to do anything." Wade said the sale of bonds in several townships in the vicinity of Triumph had been small, and apparently, he thought, "some interests have been at work offsetting the government's activities in the campaign." Although his parents came from Germany, Schwalen was born in the United States. After being charged, he was released on $1,000 bail.[5]

A few weeks later, Schwalen appeared in court before Judge E. C. Dean. He pleaded guilty to "hindering the war plans of the United States" by opposing the Liberty Loan. The indictment charged that Schwalen, when asked to buy Liberty bonds, stated, "My mother and father were born in Germany and there is German blood in me. When you strike at the German people you strike at me. I tell you there are two sides to this question" Apparently, he had a change of heart over the few days that elapsed before he appeared again before Dean for sentencing. Schwalen appeared wearing Liberty Loan and Red Cross buttons for that court date. He told the court he had subscribed to the Liberty Loan and the Red Cross. For that reason, reportedly, Dean imposed a light sentence. Schwalen was fined $100.[6]

In a round-up of alleged financial slackers and pro-Germans a delegation of citizens in Billings, Montana, headed by the "third degree" committee appointed by the Liberty Loan campaign, forced Curtis C. Oehme, a local architect to resign as a member of the Montana Board of Architectural Examiners. The mob also forced Alderman Herman Schwanz's resignation as a city council member. Accompanied by the third-degree committee, Oehme was escorted to a telegraph office where he wired his resignation to Montana Governor Sam V. Stewart. Schwanz tendered his resignation at a special meeting of the Billings City Council later in the same day that the round-up had occurred. Despite that activity, a reporter noted, "No acts of violence attended the demonstration." Oehme was alleged by members of the third-degree committee to have been guilty of pro-German utterances. He was a native of Germany and a former German soldier. In recent divorce proceedings filed in Billings, his wife accused him of strong pro-German sympathies. During the day's activities, Oehme was forced to carry an American flag through the city streets. Schwanz was accused of refusing to purchase a Liberty bond. However, it was reported that he had since subscribed to a bond. According to allegations, Edward J. Kortzeborn, proprietor of a local meat market, tore up a Liberty bond subscription blank when it was presented to him. During his seizure by the mob, he was forced to kiss the American flag and to publicly declare his allegiance to the United States in the lobby of a local hotel, to which he was escorted by the committee members. Concluded a journalist, "Members of the 'third degree' committee are leading citizens of Billings and made no effort to conceal their identities." However, nowhere in the press were their names listed.[7]

Several individuals described as "obstreperous" were brought before the Jasper County Council of Defense in Newton, Iowa, and made to explain why they disagreed with the idea they should buy bonds and why they even went so far as to make remarks such as; "To hell with the Red Cross, Y.M.C.A. and liberty loan." All of the men who were brought before the committee were not guilty of such remarks, but some were. But all were guilty of making some very strong statements of one kind and another to the various committees that harassed them over time to sign up for Liberty Loan subscriptions; the first man to be summoned before the defense council was D. A. Van Zante of Sully, Iowa. Under pressure, he had finally purchased a $1,000 bond "as per his assessment." Still, to show his contempt for the loan and the government, he had sold the bond "instantly," in the presence of many Sully business people for $800, taking a $200 loss. Those who witnessed the Van Zante transaction viewed it as an attempt to obstruct the loan. He was reported immediately to the Jasper County Council of Defense. Van Zante was notified to appear at a meeting in Newton, which he did. Fearing his action would get him into trouble; he had taken the precaution of repurchasing his bond before coming to the Newton meeting. When called upon to explain himself, he was described as "meek." After his case had been heard, he was informed that the judgment of the defense council was that he should buy $1,500 more of the bonds and donate $200 to the Red Cross and another $200 to the Army Y.M.C.A. Van Zante accepted the judgment without complaint and stated; "Gentlemen I'll do anything you say. I believe I have been in the wrong." The following case "to be tried" that day involved William Kubbernus, who had refused to accept his assessment that he purchase $1,000 worth of Liberty bonds and, instead, bought only $300 worth. After he told the council meeting the extent of his worth, it was decided to ask him to purchase an additional $1,000 worth of the bonds and to impose on Kubbernus a "fine" of $75, payable to the Red Cross and $25 to the Army Y.M.C.A.; two groups that, declared the council, were "connected with the war that had been woefully neglected by Mr. Kubbernus." That judgment was accepted entirely by Kubbernus. The third man to come before the council that day was William Korameier. He had refused to purchase a $250 bond, and, it was said, he had turned down the soliciting committee with "some rather strong language." He was asked to buy $500 worth of bonds, donate $25 to the Red Cross, and $50 to the Army Y.M.C.A. It was a decision that Korameier complied with "gladly."[8]

Before a reporter writing for a Portland, Oregon newspaper detailed cases of individual slackers in April 1918, he began his piece by stating; "The open season on slackers is noted at various places about the city where alleged seditious remarks have been made and where citizens are not slow to show their disapproval by vigorous action." Frank A. Hurte worked at the Standifer-Clarkson shipyard until he refused to buy Liberty bonds. To back up his stand, he stated that US President Woodrow Wilson bought only $1,000 worth of the bonds. At the same time, he supposedly also made an "uncomplimentary reference" to Wilson. The result of that activity was that Hurte was physically beaten up and then taken to the United States Attorney's office in Portland for investigation. Hurte was born in Germany, but he said his father became naturalized when Frank was a child. When he was detained for investigation, it was declared that; "he will probably be made to offer proof or else be interred for the war." Federal authorities in Portland were also investigating William Isensee, a "wealthy" Portland blacksmith who was said to be worth over $100,000 but would not buy Liberty bonds. "His citizenship may, perhaps, be canceled. Isensee was beaten Sat. night upon his refusal to buy bonds, coupled with his 'seditious statement'" Meanwhile, at the Portland Liberty Loan headquarters William E. Robertson, president of the Robertson Hardware and Steel Company, was declared to be a slacker because he refused to subscribe for Liberty bonds. A "large" subscription was expected from him as he was said to have made large business profits, "yet he has so far declined to prove that he is an American by buying bonds."[9]

Troubles for William Isensee had just begun. It was reported that the blacksmith and naturalized American "received a strong lesson in the primary principles of loyalty" on Wednesday, April 17, 1918, when he was fined $500 and sentenced to serve 30 days in the city jail "for disorderly conduct in resisting a committee of liberty bond solicitors" Despite a signed confession to the court that he was sorry that he took a "belligerent attitude" towards the committee that called on him on Saturday, April 13 and that he was then ready to have the committee accept his subscription for

bonds, the court handed out a severe sentence. One of the reasons
for the harshness of the sentence, it was said, was that "the sincerity
of his patriotism was questioned." In imposing the fine and jail time,
Municipal Judge Rossman told Isensee, "From the manner in which
you have answered questions here it is evident to me that you did
not mean what you said in your confession." And, added Rossman,
"It is regrettable that the penalty cannot be made as severe as when
a soldier is disrespectful to his higher officer." When he imposed the
sentence, Rossman was "applauded loudly" by the spectators in the
crowded courtroom. A room that was described as being crowded
with "loyal Americans." George G. Bowen was the leader of the group
of solicitors that called on Isensee that Saturday afternoon. He told
that court that from the moment he and his two colleagues entered
the blacksmith's office, he seemed to resent their presence and "flew
into a rage when asked to purchase a Liberty Bond." Bowen
explained that the three of them, fearing an attack of violence from
Isensee, overpowered Isensee and took him to the office of the
United States Attorney Haney. C. W. Jones, another of the three
solicitors, gave testimony that corroborated that given by Bowen.[10]

In his lengthy confession, Isensee outlined that he had been
arrested on that Saturday on behavior "growing out of my statements
and conduct toward a committee who called to see me in regard to
my subscription to some Liberty Bonds. I want to acknowledge that
I took an entirely wrong attitude toward this committee and toward
these bonds." He also gave some brief details of his background in
that confession. Isensee said he left Germany at 22 because of
military despotism, was considerably opposed to wars, and had
always been so disposed. He came to the United States some 37
years earlier [around 1880] and had lived in America since that
date. Also, he became a naturalized American citizen 26 years earlier,
renouncing any allegiance to Germany forever. He remained
opposed to war, "and this prejudice was the cause of my refusal to

buy Liberty Bonds. I see and realize now that it was an entirely unreasonable prejudice and an entirely wrong view and attitude to take, and say that without reservation or equivocation. It was really not because I was not loyal to this county. I am a loyal citizen, but I had the wrong views entirely about my duty as an American citizen toward these war measures. I realize now that I should support both, and I will support both, and I desire to place myself entirely on the right side in support of our Government in the present war." He concluded his confession by declaring, "I'm very sorry that this matter occurred and trust the committee will accept my sincere apology...no one will in the future have any occasion to question my loyalty..."[11]

The blacksmith appealed the case, and that appeal was heard in October 1918. One account of that appeal began by describing Isensee as a "German blacksmith and liberty bond slacker." While on the stand, Isensee admitted to having visited relatives in Germany in 1915 and being arrested on a charge of treason in Canada upon his return to North America. Those admissions were procured from "the reluctant witness" in Circuit Court Judge Kavanaugh's court. He also stated that those charges against him in Canada had been dismissed. Also admitted by the blacksmith was that his property was worth $50,000 but that he could not afford to buy Liberty bonds. Even if he could have afforded them, he declared he would not purchase them because of "conscientious scruples," At one point, he said to Kavanaugh, "The Government commandeers our blood; if it wants our property let it commandeer that also."[12]

On October 29, Judge Kavanaugh affirmed the conviction of Isensee. However, he reduced the fine from $500 to $50. He did so because a person could not be charged with one crime (disorderly conduct) and convicted of another (disloyalty or not buying Liberty bonds). Said Kavanaugh, "For the disloyal statements attributed to him and the statements of his attitude on the purchase of liberty bonds, as disloyal by the evidence, they will be placed in the hands of Federal officials for appropriate and effective action." The judge noted that only the federal officials had jurisdiction in those matters. Kavanaugh added; "Isensee deserves absolutely no sympathy and he should not be permitted to remain in a country he will not support in this war."[13]

In April 1918, Superior Court Judge Sweeney in Arizona received a letter from A. Mitchell Palmer, Alien Property Custodian. A little less than a year later, Palmer would be appointed United States Attorney General. That letter asked whether or not any alien property in Sweeney's county was in the hands of or controlled by the courts. All property owned by Germans was then seized in America, and the cash or the proceeds from the sale of holdings were turned into Liberty bonds "with all possible speed." At the close of the war, the property or its cash equivalent was to be returned to the aliens who owned it. The main thing, Palmer stressed in his letter, was to prevent the enemy alien from putting his assets to some use that in some way whereby the United States would be injured – such as turning money over to "Hun agents" or using it to spread propaganda."[14]

People in Tulsa, Oklahoma, and the surrounding area all "eagerly" supported the local Liberty Loan Committee, declared a reporter, who went on to state, "Reports from many towns in the vicinity show that it is exceedingly dangerous to make disloyal remarks or to even refuse to buy bonds without a mighty good reason." At a meeting in April 1918 of the Liberty bond committee of Collinsville, Oklahoma, the names of area residents David Goyette, W. L. Candle, Jack Schafer, and the Reverend Sallee were all read out as financial slackers. Only the prompt action, it was said, of John M. Goldesberry, a prominent attorney, and James D. Ward, president of an oil company, prevented summary punishment being meted out to the men who had been named. However, in the early morning of Thursday, April 11, "parties" called at the Candle residence and took him downtown to his butcher shop. When they arrived at the store, they tore up his fixtures, overturned the counters, and broke the shop windows. Candle's reason for not purchasing a bond was that his wife had control of the business and the money and would not allow him to make such a purchase. The interior of a furniture store owned by Goyette was daubed with yellow paint. Goyette was described in this account as a Socialist and a former president of the Collinsville City Council. According to Collinsville reports, Jack Schafer had never shown "a decided amount of patriotism," and was simply told to buy a bond, which he did. The Reverend Sallee had been preaching at the Holy Roller Church on the evils of war. He was forced to stop preaching and to "quit the neighborhood." Another man, unnamed but said to be "well-known" in the city, was "arrested" under an order of the County Council of Defense on April 11 when he reportedly said to Liberty bond salesmen, "go to hell," when they called upon him and asked him to increase his purchase of bonds. Finally, on April 11, a merchant who ran a store in the area refused to purchase a bond, although he owned "good property." A committee went out to see him, and "his indifference to the country impressed them as approaching so closely to disloyalty that they gave him an unmerciful drubbing."[15]

At an April 1918 meeting of the New York City Board of Aldermen, a resolution offered by vice-chairman Robert Moran passed. That resolution urged upon the people of New York City the importance of responding promptly and generously to the call of the United States Government for subscriptions to the Third Liberty loan campaign. According to the article, "The seven Socialist members [of the board], who were threatened with violence at a previous meeting when they opposed the war savings stamps campaign, voted for the resolution. One of those Socialist aldermen was Algernon Lee.[16]

That violence mentioned above took place at a February 27 meeting of the same board. Physical violence did not take place; it stopped with words. Words used against Lee, as the spokesman for the seven Socialist aldermen, included "traitor," "coward," "dog," "definitely disloyal," and "American Bolsheviki." The fuss was over the seven Socialists' discouragement of the sale of War Savings Stamps. C. P. Wiley, representing the National War Savings Committee, had addressed the board, asking it to push the stamp sales. When such a resolution was introduced, the Socialist alderman all opposed it. Said Lee, "We hold that the cost of war should be placed on wealth accumulated by crushing the poorest people. The war savings stamp is virtually an indirect tax on the poorest people, virtual coercion of the most helpless part of the population...We do not oppose this thing, but we do not join in it." Those remarks led to a storm of outrage on the part of the other aldermen. One who expressed his fury was William P. Kenneally, who invited Lee to step into a side room where, said Kenneally, Lee would either kiss the American flag or be thrown from a window. Lee declined to accept the challenge. Shaking his fist at the Socialist spokesman, Kenneally thundered, "What's wanted in this city is a patriotic committee that will use the rope on every disloyal person...I would not hesitate for one minute to commit deliberate murder of any man who is a traitor to the flag." Hours later, a meeting of the Committee on Rules was held to consider and discuss the idea of expelling all seven of the Socialists from the Board of Aldermen. However, it was decided not to proceed, but only on the matter of a technicality. Because no official stenographer had been in attendance at the meeting, no official record of the events existed. Any expulsion could be appealed to the courts, and with no official record of proceedings, it was felt that no court would sustain an expulsion. The only result was the resolve to introduce a resolution at the next board meeting that an official stenographer should be provided at all board sessions.[17]

In Arizona, Judge A. C. Lockwood of the Superior Court of Cochise County told W. E. Schwamm of Douglas, Arizona, a prospective jury member, "You can go home," following the refusal by citizens of Douglas to sit on the same jury with Schwamm The Douglas citizens explained that Schwamm had refused to buy bonds of the Third Liberty issue. Schwamm declared that he had purchased a small bond of the Second Liberty issue. Said Lockwood; "Mr. Schwamm, you came to Douglas a poor man You made to the knowledge of the court and old-timers of Douglas, large sums, much of which you still have either in property or money. In the present emergency, you say you cannot help the government. I do not blame these citizens of Douglas who say they cannot sit on a jury with you."[18]

An editor with an Arizona newspaper was moved by the Schwamm case to comment; "Slowly but surely public sentiment is being crystallized, and the time will come when the slacker will call for the rocks and mountains to fall on him, that there might not be left a trace or recollection of one so vile as to refuse to respond to his country's call. Verily, the slacker will find he has yet ahead of him a rough and rocky road."[19]

Another editor of a different Arizona newspaper penned a lengthy editorial and began by observing that "patriotic" citizens of Douglas and Judge A. C. Lockwood "deserve no little praise from the public for the manner in which they dealt with a Liberty Loan slacker..." when he appeared in Tombstone for jury duty. With respect to the complaints from fellow jury members who refused to sit with Schwamm because he refused to buy bonds, this editor said, "The court accepted their evidence, took the offending juror's statement, and ordered his name stricken from the jury list." In dismissing the "offender the court used language which only a patriotic American could use, and with which every patriotic American agreed. The jurors remaining applauded." Added

Lockwood, "I do not blame these citizens of Douglas who say they cannot sit on a jury with you. The court does not consider that you are a decent American citizen, fit to sit on the jury, and you are discharged from service on the jury and your name will be stricken from the jury list." In his conclusion the editor declared Schwamm "had received the just punishment due him. Men with whom he had lived for fifteen years and among whom he had thrived had declined to be associated with him. His refusal to aid the government had been aired in the public court room. His denunciation was complete. The shame which was heaped upon him had been brought about by himself. It was the greatest of all shames – the brand of slacker, of un-Americanism...He had been disowned by a community which had formerly honored and loved him." The editor added, "Every Liberty Bond slacker should take this lesson to heart...Money in times of war can purchase the honor and respect of a community, for every man who assists the government wholeheartedly, will receive the blessing of his fellow citizens. But money withheld from the vaults of war can cost its owner what money can never purchase – love, friendship and close personal and business relations which only time and hard labor of years can create, build up and cement."[20]

William E. Schwamm was dismissed from jury service on April 18, 1918, and was arrested on the afternoon of April 20 by Justin Daspit of the United States Department of Justice. He was held on $10,000 bail, which was posted for him. Schwamm was accused of violating the Espionage Act by making "seditious utterances." The specific charges were not revealed then and would not be until the accused appeared for a preliminary hearing before United States Commissioner H. C. Beumler. At this time, it was also reported that Schwamm had not bought a bond directly during the Second Liberty campaign but had taken a $50 bond from a workman who owed Schwamm $40. Nothing more was reported on this case.[21]

Some reports of force and violence used against financial slackers were brief and sketchy. One such was a report in April 1918 that reported that for the offense of refusing to purchase a Liberty bond, Ira Schroeder, employed by the John A. Roebling Sons Company in Trenton, New Jersey, "was rudely handled by other workmen."[22]

Around the same time, "Loyalty Leaguers" in the Pittsburgh, Pennsylvania area, who had conducted numerous "tar and feather parties" during the previous week, had reportedly caused "no little worry to alien enemies in this community." Many organizations had been springing up in the mill districts to "handle foreigners who denounce the Allies and the Liberty Loan. Within twenty-four hours twelve tar and feather parties have been carried out in the vicinity of Pittsburgh." One such victim was "Joe" Barlok, a 30-year-old German from Beaver, Pennsylvania, who was tarred and feathered because of alleged disloyal remarks against the Third Liberty Loan. Three unnamed Austrians who made derogatory remarks concerning the loan were tarred and feathered at Woodlawn, a short distance from Pittsburgh. Two Austrians and one Italian were rolled in black paint and "roughly handled" by employees of the McClintic-Marshall Construction Company when they refused to buy bonds.[23]

A report from San Francisco observed that 500 employees of the Southern Pacific Railroad, led by a brass band, took three of their fellow employees out of the rail yard after the three had failed to buy Liberty bonds. Wooden signs with the word "slackers" were carried at the head of the procession. After the brief march, the crowd released the three men. Then it staged an unscheduled campaign at which $2,000 worth of Liberty bonds were subscribed, bringing the total for the "loyalists" who worked at Southern Pacific to $60,000 worth of bonds.[24]

It was reported from Arlington, South Dakota, that August Lieske "is the only man in this part of Kingsbury County who would not buy Liberty Bonds. On account of his abundant means this did not look right." Then on the night of April 20, 1918, at around 10 PM, a crowd of about 100 men with a large quantity of yellow paint visited his farm on the outskirts of Arlington and "decorated" his house, barn, chicken coop, and even the trees and fence posts. A cartoonist in the crowd also designed two pictures of the German Kaiser, which he affixed in yellow paint to the Lieske residence. Remarked a journalist, "Lieske is to be given another opportunity to buy Liberty Bonds and if he still refuses he is to be more severely dealt with."[25]

Because he refused to buy Liberty bonds during a campaign at the Atchison, Topeka, and Santa Fe Railway shops in Las Vegas, New Mexico, Louis A. Lee was branded with a coat of yellow paint before a crowd of about 500 people. That crowd was headed by J. S. Christal, with various shopmen officiating at the "ceremony." On the yellow coat Lee wore were the words "Liberty Loan Slacker." Christal assisted Lee into the yellow garment and addressed those present, explaining the reason for the action. When the bond drive started at the Santa Fe shop several days earlier, Lee was among those not initially solicited. Then when he was finally approached and urged to subscribe, he refused "emphatically," and on several subsequent approaches, he also refused to buy. That led to a report that the ire of the "entire plant" was raised against him. A meeting was held, and it was decided a committee should approach him and ask him, once again, to purchase bonds. That committee did so but was told by Lee that he had already bought $500 worth of bonds. However, an investigation proved that to be incorrect, and the committee went back to see Lee yet again. That return visit disclosed to the committee that Lee had not been "sincere" and had not purchased any bonds. And that led to more drastic action on the part of his fellow employees.[26]

On the evening of April 21, 1918, large signs were erected on several private and business properties in Hibbing, Minnesota. The town turned out the ore for the Gary, Indiana, steel mills. That sign read, "I refused to buy Liberty bonds." A crowd of around 200 men went to a hotel and placed the sign in front of the property. Then an identical sign was placed on several house fronts in the town. According to the reporter, "When those in the homes and the owners of the hotel buy bonds the signs will be taken down."[27]

Another example of the use of force took place in Steelton, Pennsylvania, a part of greater Harrisburg. Employees of a machine shop in that community, declared a journalist, "displaying their determination to rid the local steel plant of all unpatriotic foreigners," bound Kaspar Hartick, an Austrian, with a rope and prepared to throw him in the old Pennsylvania canal because he refused "point blank" to subscribe to a Liberty bond. The men in the mob were persuaded to free Hartick by officials of the plant after they had carried out part of their plans to punish the "disloyal" worker; "Although the foreigner was not thrown into the canal he was badly treated and received lacerations and bruises of the face and body," it was said in the account. The following morning, officials at that steel plant stated that Hartick had been discharged after the incident. The police department conducted an investigation "and found that some of the reports of the incident were greatly exaggerated," said those officials. It was said to be unknown how long Hartick had worked at the plant and whether or not he was a naturalized American citizen. One unnamed steelworker said, "I went to Hartick on Saturday and asked him to buy a bond. He said he did not want to buy any. I told him to think it over until Monday, that during that time he may change his mind." When he approached Hartick a day later, the latter reiterated that he did not wish to buy any bonds; "Not being able to do much with him I went to a fellow worker and sent him to see Hartick." At that point, he allegedly said, "Damn the Liberty Loan." That refusal circulated through the plant, and workers at once decided to impress upon Hartick's mind what they thought of such actions. He was bound and marched through the shop. As he was paraded thus, the crowd accumulated, and by the time they reached the plant door, the group was composed of about 150 workmen, all work colleagues of the victim. At that point, factory supervisors persuaded the men to release their prisoner; he was taken to the office and escorted from the plant by the police. "It is reported that when the men were taking Hartick through the plant, he would try to hold them back by holding fast to car wheels and other obstructions. He would release his grasp when struck on the arms by workmen." It was also noted that; "After Hartick saw the workmen meant to punish him for his leanings, it is understood, he said he would subscribe but by then the workmen told him it was too late."[28]

Walter Cooperider was a farmer of German extraction who lived nine miles southwest of McPherson, Kansas. He was tarred and feathered by a mob because of allegedly disloyal remarks made by him and because he was also listed as a bond slacker. His father, T. J. Cooperider, 90 years old and bedridden for the previous year, was made to kiss the American flag. The identity of the members of the mob was said to be unknown. A well-known banker who lived in the area explained that one night he met a party of about 40 men grouped around some 15 cars parked near the Cooperider home. Curious as to why the men were there, he stopped his car to investigate, but he was told by the mob to "move on," He did so and declared that because of the darkness, he did not recognize any members of the mob.[29]

Late in April 1918, five Austrians refused to purchase Liberty bonds at the Lyttle colliery near Pottsville, Pennsylvania. As a result, they were taken by the heels by other workmen, dragged some distance, and then dipped into a steel tank used for storing heating oil. The result, remarked a reporter, was that; "The men are today covered with an amber stain that will not wash off. They all purchased bonds today."[30]

Even wealthier men fell victim to the bond patriots. A group of men reportedly residing "somewhere in the west" had forfeited a national bank charter because of failure to subscribe "liberally" to the bond campaigns. Local bankers were said to have been discussing the story for several days in Omaha, Nebraska. Rumor had it that the incident "relates closely to Nebraska, although none here is in position to give names of men or place." The story reached a broader audience when it was given out as a circular letter to bankers from the office of the comptroller of the currency in Washington, dated April 20. When the comptroller investigated the paperwork for a new national bank charter, "doubt arose as to the loyalty and patriotism of the applicants, and it was ascertained that, although the six applicants for the charter were reported to be men of considerable means – several of them claiming to be worth $250,000 or more – the aggregate amount of Liberty bonds of the first and second issues to which the six applicants had subscribed was only $200, several of the applicants for the charter having no Liberty bonds at all, and their aggregate subscriptions to the Red Cross had been only $149." Thus, explained the story, the application for a new national bank was rejected "on the ground that men of means in these times, who show so little patriotism and so little public spirit in the matter of making subscriptions to Liberty bonds and to the Red Cross, are unfit to be placed in charge of any national bank."[31]

On an April day in 1918, at the Monitor Stove and Range Company plant in Kentucky, three men "employed at good wages" refused to purchase Liberty bonds because their religious beliefs opposed contributions of any kind having to do with war. The other

120 molders employed at that plant had "patriotically" purchased the bonds. It was reported that the "three blasphemers who had used religion as a cloak to hide either their pro-Germanism or their penuriousness or both, were discharged by H. L. Gorsuch, a company official." In an editorial about the incident, the newspaperman said he wanted "to congratulate Mr. Gorsuch for this prompt and wholesome exhibition of Americanism." The editor argued that, with respect to defeating the Kaiser, "it will help mightily if all concerns...should 'can' the slackers, be they bond slackers, service slackers or what not."[32]

Near Wilkes-Barre, Pennsylvania, some 200 men employed in the Ashley Pennsylvania shops of the Central Railroad led Adam Milbroadt out of the shop with a rope around his neck. He was told to buy a Liberty bond, or he would be strung up. Then he was led to a bank in the community where he did indeed purchase a Liberty bond. Milbroadt was a German and had caused it to be known at the plant that he had bought no bonds of either the first or second issue and that he did not intend to buy any of the third issue bonds. Workmen called on him the day before they turned into a mob and asked him to subscribe, but Milbroadt bluntly refused. The following day, the mob had him on the end of a rope and dragged him from the shop. Reportedly they were looking for a tree from which to hang him, declaring he deserved no mercy when Milbroadt agreed to buy a bond. To give him a chance to fulfill his promise, the mob led and dragged him to the only bank in Ashley, where he subscribed for a $500 bond. The same news item carried a brief mention to the effect that Mike Bruie, and Steve Brosut, Austrians, were taken from their work in the Mineral Springs, Pennsylvania colliery and tarred and feathered because they refused to buy Liberty bonds.[33]

In Denison, Texas, the places of business of some firms classed as slacker institutions were painted in huge yellow letters during the night, and the following day passersby saw the word "slacker" in large yellow letters on the storefronts.[34]

When supposed slackers found themselves on the wrong end of paint brushes, that paint was almost always yellow, even though equating yellow with cowardice made no sense with respect to financial slackers. Yellow paint, "and plenty of it," according to a news report, was spread over the front of the home of August Kubath 803 Elm Street, in Atlantic Iowa. He was, continued the report, "what is commonly termed a slacker, having refused to purchase a Liberty bond or contribute to any of the many war activities though amply able to do so." Kubath's house was not only well painted. Still, it was also tagged with signs and inscriptions such as "Buy a liberty bond before Wednesday night," Buy liberty bonds within twenty-four hours," and "Every miser helps the kaiser." An American flag was also attached to the front of the house. Kubath had been employed at the Shrauger and Johnson plant but was immediately discharged by the company after the painting incident; supposedly, that firing was because of Kubath's "pro-Germanism."[35]

When the colliery committee called on Edward Harris, employed at the number one colliery of the Susquehanna Coal Company, and urged the Wilkes-Barre Pennsylvania resident to subscribe for a Liberty bond, "He refused to listen to pleadings and also to threats," according to a reporter. Thereupon a score of men procured a rope, placed a noose around his neck, and dragged him to the timber yard, where the rope was pulled over timber several feet above his head. Tightening the rope, so he was forced to stand on the tips of his toes, Harris was asked whether he had changed his mind about bonds. He faintly declared that he had indeed and that he would buy a bond. He was released by the mob and was to be allowed to keep his promise.[36]

The raising of a new American flag late in April 1918 at the factory of the St. Johns Rubber Company, located in the St. Johns neighborhood of Portland, Oregon, was the occasion of the unmasking of an alleged American slacker concerning the buying of Liberty bonds. The unnamed individual was seized by fellow employees and hustled outside the gates. He was told that he had better look for another job. However, reflection convinced the man that his attitude was wrong, and he lost no time in buying, for cash, one $100 bond and in purchasing on the installment plan a second $100 bond. As well noted a journalist, "He took an oath of allegiance and kissed the flag."[37]

Because he refused to buy Liberty bonds or assist the Red Cross, George Geanaputos, a confectioner at Electra, 30 miles north of Wichita Falls, Texas, was taken to the edge of town by 23 businessmen, tarred and feathered and escorted out of town.[38]

Bond slackers in the area of Wilkes-Barre, Pennsylvania, came under attack yet again in April 1918. Mason Cragle, a politician in Plymouth Township, was taken from his duties at the Avondale mine and had a rope placed around his neck. That rope was slung over a tree limb, and Cragle was saved from possible death when he pleaded a willingness to buy a $1,000 bond. In another incident in the area, miners of the South Wilkes-Barre colliery of Lehigh and Wilkes Barre Coal Company declared they would refuse to work unless Walter Meadows, a shift engineer, bought a Liberty bond or was fired from his job.[39]

Late on the night of Wednesday, April 24, 1918, a group of men defaced the barn on the C. M. Pederson farm in Boyer Township, Iowa, by printing the word "slacker" on it in several different places. A sign that measured three to four square feet was nailed on his mailbox post bearing the words "C. M. Pederson, worth $30,000 bought $250 worth of bonds – Slacker." The members of the Boyer

Township Council of Defense were reported "up in arms" when they learned of this "depredation" on Thursday morning and called a meeting to investigate. The township council felt an injustice had been done to Pederson "inasmuch as he had subscribed for the amount of bonds which they had set as his share of the township quota and had subscribed liberally to the kindred war funds that had been raised." Following an investigation late into the night on that Thursday, council members drove to Denison, Iowa, at midnight and swore out an information against one David Selden, charging him with malicious mischief and trespassing on the property of Pederson. Deputy Sheriff Costello arrested Selden on Friday. When he appeared before Justice Rollins, he waived the preliminary hearing and was bound over to await the action of the grand jury, which was scheduled to meet in September. He was released on Saturday after having furnished a cash bond of $500. Selden was formerly employed by Pederson, but a short time earlier, he was discharged by Pederson. After being fired, Selden made his home with a brother-in-law who resided a short distance from the Pederson home. Members of the Council of Defense found paint corresponding in color to that used on the Pederson barn in a shed on the property where Selden was staying, and a jacket owned by Selden was found smeared with paint of the same color. Selden proclaimed his innocence when he appeared before Justice Rollins.[40]

Sitting in a jail cell in Los Angeles at the beginning of May 1918 was Peter Blankstrom, described as a "Norseman." He was charged with being a Liberty loan slacker and having made "unpatriotic" remarks about the ability of the United States government to carry out its promises.[41]

Reverend John Haefner, the pastor of the German Lutheran Church in Muscatine, Iowa, was the central figure in what was described as a "patriotic demonstration" in Muscatine on May 1, 1918, which came as a conclusion to a luncheon held at the Hotel

Muscatine where a former German naval officer gave a "patriotic address." While the speaking was in progress, a "delegation" of citizens visited the Haefner home and requested that the minister accompany them. Shortly after 1:00 PM, the home guard formed a procession that included a band and businessmen and marched Haefner through the downtown streets. A number of the paraders carried signs expressive of the sentiment actuating the demonstration. Some of these read; "Mr. Bond Slacker you're Next;" "100 per cent Americanism breeds confidence;" and "German instruction means English destruction." A sign was affixed to the back of Haefner that read; "If you don't like to speak the English language use signs" Dr. A. J. Oliver addressed the crowd when the parade, with Haefner, reached city hall where, said a journalist; "It is also a custom to make the disloyal kneel and kiss the flag, but we think that he has suffered sufficient humiliation." Oliver told Haefner, "If you do not believe that this is your country and our flag is you flag, you had better go back to Germany and the sooner the better. There isn't a person in Muscatine but that would be glad to see you go." Several people in the crowd replied, "Amen." According to the account, Haefner was led to his car "and returned safely to his home. The crowd dispersed quickly and quietly and no attempt was made to molest the minister as he was led to the car."[42]

One day later, the Reverend Haefner was charged with desecrating the American flag in an information filed by Dr. Oliver. The flag was one that had been presented to the minister by a body of citizens some weeks earlier. The belief was that Haefner failed to display the "proper respect" for the flag. On May 11, Haefner was acquitted on the charge of desecrating the American flag, with the jury being out in deliberations for just 40 minutes. It appeared that sometime earlier, an American flag put up in front of Haefner's house fell from its socket and lay for "quite a while on the ground." It was that incident that led to the charge of desecration. During this time,

Haefner also remedied his bond deficiencies. The assistant cashier of a Muscatine bank testified that Haefner had bought a $100 bond and arranged to buy a $50 bond. The bank also reported that it had received $22 from the clergyman for the Red Cross. Members of his congregation testified their pastor had urged them at a Sunday service to purchase Liberty bonds.[43]

An article in a Kansas newspaper pointed out that if a boy called in the draft hid out and failed to appear when his name was called, "everyone would point at him the finger of scorn – a Slacker." Yet, the journalist argued, there were people in the town "ten times worse slackers than such a boy would be." He wondered if it was not the case that the draft evading boy had more extenuating circumstances "than the man who had rather loan his money out at ten per cent to individuals than to buy Liberty Bonds at a lower rate of interest." In the first instance, the boy was asked to give up everything worthwhile, including perhaps his life. In the latter case, all that was asked was a temporary financial sacrifice, "and when men refuse to do this the good name of the community is at stake. This town should be too big a place to permit slackers to hide within its confines. The man who has the money and will not buy Liberty Bonds is just as dangerous as the Boche [German soldier] in the trenches – even more so. The known German sympathizer can be watched – can be shot, but there is no law to reach the Liberty Bond slacker unless patriotic citizens invest in yellow paint and chicken feathers." The journalist declared, "We want to go on record as being hostile to such [slackers]. We are ashamed to live in the same community with them. Where would Seward County be today if everyone were like them – in the slacker class, despised by every Liberty-loving American citizen, and justly so. The Slacker should not be tolerated." Nonetheless, the newspaperman stated Seward County was over its quota for bond subscriptions and "we take off our hat to the Real Americans and wish we had words strong enough to express our contempt for the miserable slackers. We know who they are and we are almost in the notion of publishing their names and pedigrees as some other papers are doing."[44]

Josef Knitig, a wealthy farmer from Decatur County, Kansas, was approached by the local Liberty bond committee and asked to subscribe to some bonds. Knitig informed the committee at Oberlin, Kansas that there was "no law to make him buy Liberty Bonds." But one day later, it was reported, "Not only did he buy a Liberty bond but he led a procession through the town and carried a flag." He also apologized to the town for his previous attitude. A newspaper editor commented on this incident by writing, "Where Mr. Knitig made a mistake was in relying upon the fact that there was no law to 'make' him do what the public sentiment of his community felt that he should do." Had there been a law on the subject, thought the editor, "Mr. Knitig could have employed a lawyer, applied for an injunction, filed a demurrer, taken an appeal, moved for a new trial, asked for an amended petition, moved to make the charges more definite and specific, invoked the constitution." Concluded the editor; "Under our system of jurisprudence and technical court rules, Mr. Knitig could have found plenty of loopholes to escape doing the thing the law would 'make' him do. But public opinion pays mighty little attention to technicalities."[45]

But for the timely appearance of Vincent Schindel, manager of the Carbon County Liberty Loan Committee, four alleged loan slackers would have received rough treatment from a mob of zinc workers in Palmerton, Pennsylvania. Schindel learned of the plan to wreak vengeance upon a clerk in Palmerton and three "well-to-do" men at Little Gap, Pennsylvania, four miles away, and was able to avert any violence by selling bonds to all of the men. An area "vigilant committee" with 18 automobiles, 100 men, and armed with ropes were passing the Palmerton main mine office on their way to Little Gap when they were stopped by a telephone message and told by

Schindel that the intended victims had complied with the committee and subscribed to bonds. Other slackers in the same area were also targeted at the same time. A man employed at the New Jersey Zinc Works at Hazard, Pennsylvania, who refused to buy a Liberty bond was about to be thrown in the Lehigh Canal by fellow employees when his clothing was searched, and money sufficient to buy a Liberty Bond was found. He was spared the involuntary bath by being convinced to invest the money in a bond. Another man was suspended from a crane and about to be plunged into a barrel of tar when he also agreed to purchase a bond. Grant Walck, a farmer residing in the area at Aquashicola, Pennsylvania, was threatened by a mob with hanging unless he agreed to buy a Liberty bond. He loaded his gun and defied anyone to carry out that threat. At that point, the mob withdrew. Walck said the reason he did not buy a bond was that he could not afford it. However, he later arranged to purchase a bond and did so.[46]

John Knight worked as a moulder at the plant of the Wheeling Mould and Foundry Company in West Virginia, where shrapnel shells were being manufactured for the United States government and said a news account, "narrowly missed lynching because of his refusal to buy a Liberty Bond." However, cooler heads prevailed, and no violence ensued, although a rope had been secured by the mob, and preparations had been made for the lynching. Instead, Knight's fellow employees notified the plant management they would strike unless Knight was discharged. It was reported that the management of the plant "commended the patriotic spirit of its employees and discharged Knight."[47]

Two unnamed employees of a railroad shop in Las Vegas, Nevada, suspected by their fellow workmen of being Liberty Loan slackers, were tied to a post and soaked with water from a hose. Then yellow paint was poured over them, and they were turned loose with instructions not to return to Las Vegas. However, upon investigation, it was found that one of the men had bought a bond in his wife's name, and the other man was deeply in debt because of his wife's long illness. According to the account, "The men are now endeavoring to make reparations for their action," although no details were given.[48]

Newton Peterman, a Glenn County California rancher, whose wealth was said to be "conservatively" estimated at $150,000, was, on a day in May 1918, called a man without a county as the result of action taken a few days earlier by a group of 26 "prominent" members of the Glenn County Liberty Loan Committee, after they adopted resolutions accepting a proposition made by Peterman if his "forced" subscription of $600 to the Third Liberty Loan campaign was not acceptable. Peterman was requested to leave the county, and every merchant in the county was requested not to have business or social dealings with him. The action was taken by the Glenn County committee after Peterman had been urged on several occasions to buy Liberty bonds in keeping with his financial means. He admitted to the group that he had made $50,000 on the previous year's crop and had $14,000 in cash in Glenn County banks. He said his 1,100-acre ranch was assessed for $34,500, but he would take only a single $100 bond. The committee refused that subscription, so he bought it at the bank, then the committee called a meeting to deal with his case. Word of the proposed meeting reached Peterman, and he rushed to the bank and purchased an additional $500 subscription, and then remarked, "If the committee doesn't like this I will leave the county." Peterman was requested to appear at the meeting to explain his case, but he failed to present himself. Because of that non-appearance, the Glenn County Liberty Loan Committee passed two resolutions to dispose of the case. The first resolution declared, "That it is the sense of this committee that the proposition so advanced by said Newton Peterman (that he leave the county) be accepted and that he be notified that the liberty loving patriotic people of Glenn county would be well pleased to have him move from the County of Glenn." The second resolution stated, "We recommend to the merchants and to all patriotic people generally that they abstain from association of any kind with said Newton Peterman to the extent that they shall refuse to have any commercial dealings with him or to his use or for his benefit, or any association with any merchant or other person who does have commercial dealing with said Newton Peterman, or to his use or benefit." The members of the Liberty Loan Committee present at the meeting which adopted the resolutions numbered 26 – all of whom were named in the newspaper article.[49]

Two days later, it was noted that in addition to not buying enough bonds, Peterman also was not a member of the Red Cross and refused to join the War Work League. He was placed on a boycott list by Willows California (county seat of Glenn County) by the Willows War Work League and town merchants. Peterman had, reportedly, moved with his furniture and family "to parts as yet unknown," and his ranch was sold to E. E. Willard, formerly of Portland, Oregon.[50]

The First National Bank in Pasadena, California, wrote a letter to one of its depositors in May 1918. That letter said, "Dear Sir; We hold at the present time about $60,000 worth of first mortgages belonging to you, on which we collect payments for you. We have held as high as $90,000 of these. We know that you own stock here and real estate in Iowa, that make you a wealthy man. You are what the bank describes as a good customer, and we are indebted to you for past business." The letter continued, "You have not subscribed to either first, second or third Liberty Loans. You are not a member of the Red Cross and, so far as we know, are not supporting your country in any way." That letter, signed by J. S. MacDonnell, cashier, added, "You are not only a detriment, but a menace to this community. This bank cannot afford to thrive on business such as yours. We have too many calls from patriotic citizens these days to be willing to extend credit to you in order that you may reinvest at from 7 per cent up. You will therefore, please take up your small note of $300 immediately, also call at the bank and receipt for your securities, and take your business to some bank that has money to lend to German sympathizers." In connection with the letter, MacDonnell announced that "in any further extension of credit the bank will make the purchase or non purchase of Liberty Bonds a consideration;" that is, for all customers.[51]

A general boycott against every member of organized labor discovered to be a Liberty bond slacker was ordered by the Central Labor Council executive committee of San Jose, California. The council maintained there could only be two reasons for the failure to subscribe to the loan. Those reasons were financial inability or disloyalty. A committee from the union was to inquire into the financial condition of those who did not buy bonds and to list them as slackers if they could buy bonds but had not done so. According to a resolution passed and adopted, all other union men were to refuse to work with slackers until they bought bonds.[52]

Mine company employees ran into problems in Arizona at around the same time, all because they did not contribute to the Red Cross in its war efforts. A Red Cross slacker was ridden on a rail from the Junction mine (near Bisbee). One day later, two more "of the same type received the same treatment." At the mine at Holbrook, Arizona, a man was almost hanged for refusing to donate to the Red Cross. And finally, an employee of a large store was discharged for a similar refusal. However, it was said that miners, in general, were praised for their purchase of war stamps and Liberty bonds.[53]

On Monday, May 27, 1918, the citizens of Bisbee, Arizona, went to the polls to select a mayor and six aldermen to govern their community. On the day before the election, a page one editorial appeared in a Bisbee newspaper. That editorial declared that only one significant issue was involved – that issue was patriotism – and that "party lines have been practically discarded..." The candidates running in opposition to the Citizens' Non-partisan ticket had come before the voters, said the editor, "under a false flag." Their record with respect to the purchase of Liberty bonds had been published in this newspaper. In brief, the record showed that the six candidates had purchased, in the three Liberty bond campaigns to that date, a total of just $550 worth of bonds for all six of them. It showed further that candidates Acord, Newberry, and Foudy had purchased no bonds at all, despite being financially able to do so. Another candidate, Walsh, owned one $100 bond from the First Liberty campaign but nothing from the Second and Third Loan drive. Moreover, not one of the candidates had even taken part in campaigns for Liberty bonds, War Savings Stamps, or the Red Cross, and they had given nothing of their time or energy to other government agencies such as the food administration. On the other side of the ledger were the six candidates for aldermen on the Citizens' Non-partisan ticket. Those men had purchased $21,750 worth of Liberty bonds in the three campaigns, and all six had done other "patriotic" work. As far as this editor was concerned, the voters of Bisbee "are offered two selections – the one selfish, self-centered slackers – the other patriotic citizens." Concluded the editor; "And when the votes are counted Monday night the reply of the citizens of Bisbee to this flagrant, insulting request for support of Liberty bond slackers, will be written in the overwhelming victory of the Citizens' non-partisan ticket." And, just as the editor predicted, all six men on the Citizens' Non-partisan ticket won. Four won very easily in run-away contests, while the other two were victorious in somewhat more closely contested races.[54]

When people were forced to buy Liberty bonds, one could argue that the victim did not suffer any loss as he would eventually get his money back, with an interest rate that was close to, but a little short of, the going rate at the time for savings accounts in the banks. However, such an argument could not be advanced when people were forced to give money to the Red Cross or some other "patriotic" group doing war work. That money was a donation and would not be recovered. Hart Duxbury, a farmer who lived near Spencer, South Dakota, was tarred and feathered in May 1918 by 50 farmers in the same area after being taken from his farm to the jail at Spencer, where the coat of tar and the feathers was applied. Duxbury, it was said, was ordered on a Friday night to purchase bonds or contribute to the Red Cross by the following Monday night. He refused, and the farmers made good on their threat.[55]

George Hydeck, Marion Minersky, Frank Sorrocco, and John Noonan were the only miners employed by the Pennsylvania Coal and Coke Company at Marstellar, Pennsylvania, near Johnstown, who refused to contribute a day's wages to the Red Cross. When the four men left work one evening, the other 300 men employed in the mine, said a news item, "captured them at the mine opening, stripped them to the waist and liberally applied tar and feathers, afterward parading them through the town." According to the report, "no further violence was attempted, but the miners in the mob said they would not go to work on the following morning unless the four men were fired if they saw fit to show up at the mine.[56]

About 40 citizens armed with brushes and yellow paint went on a collection tour for Red Cross contributions (for their war work) on the night of May 27, 1918, in Sharon, Wisconsin, and two houses in the area were marred with many yellow crosses. George Dillam, a wealthy farmer who had given $5 to the Red Cross earlier, made an additional midnight contribution of $15. As a result, his residence was spared a coat of yellow paint. John Westphal, described as an "enemy alien," who had already purchased $1,800 of Liberty bonds, a collection of thrift stamps, and had a receipt for $1 donated to the Red Cross, complained to the mob that he had no more money left to give. Nonetheless, his house was given an unwanted paint job. M. W. Chapman, a wealthy civil war veteran, refused to donate any money, and his house also received a redecoration.[57]

D. P. Kenyon was an Ely, Nevada resident who worked at McGill, Nevada. On a Monday afternoon, he was surrounded by a crowd of fellow workmen as he came off shift and "was ridden on a rail through the streets of the smelter city and repeatedly ducked in a water trough, after which he was told to leave the camp," declared a reporter. The cause of the feeling against him was that he refused to subscribe to a Liberty Loan bond or to contribute even a small amount to the Red Cross and "the further fact that he made slurring remarks against the Red Cross." After being repeatedly ducked into the water, the mob took photos of him that the mob intended to sell for the benefit of the Red Cross. "The sentiment of the community of McGill, and in fact throughout the entire district, is strongly with the men who administered the punishment," added the journalist. "There may be reasons for a man's failure to purchase Liberty bonds, but surely no man, with a single spark of patriotism who is drawing a good salary can give a good reason for not contributing something to the noble work of the Red Cross..." And the newsman concluded, "A man who can, but refused to aid in such a cause, should not be recognized by his fellow workers and neighbors."[58]

Fifteen lashes across his bare back and legs and the application of a coat of tar and feathers was the sentence pronounced by C. F. Rose, chairman of the Council of Defense of Hooker Oklahoma, in the "trial" of B. W. Maris for calling the Red Cross an institution for graft "and not having backbone enough to protect his wife and family from ravishing Huns if they required it." Maris was a farmer who lived in the Hardesty district, 18 miles south of Hooker. He had made several statements in regard to the Red Cross being an institution of graft and stated publicly that he would not donate to the Red Cross. As well he refused to sign a loyalty pledge. After receiving the coat of tar and feathers, he was escorted to the city limits and told never to cross again the line leading into the city of Hooker.[59]

Angelo Perez was, as of June 1918, a resident and property owner in the Bisbee, Arizona, area and had been so for some ten years. On a day in early June, he was made "the guest of honor" in a Red Cross parade through the Warren district of Bisbee. Following the parade, he was thrown into a water tank, pulled out of the tank, rolled in the mud, returned to the district on the radiator of a truck, and forced to eat several pounds of "Liberty sausage." Several times during the incident, Perez was forced to kiss a large Red Cross flag that adorned the truck in the presence of large audiences. Across his chest, placed there while he was attached to the radiator of the truck, was a large banner bearing the inscription "Red Cross slacker." He was made to stand in front of the post office in Bisbee while a spokesman told the audience of his refusal to contribute to the Red Cross. Perez was then made to kiss the Red Cross banner on the truck again. About six vehicles, filled with men and women, made up the procession to start, but the number reached about 50 vehicles later in the procession; "Cowbells, horns, motor horns and other means of making noise, attracted the crowds to the parade and told of the Perez punishment." At the close of the procession, Perez was asked if he wished to contribute to the Red Cross. His reply was an "eager" affirmative, and he handed over $25. He had earlier pledged to contribute to the organization but then complained when the amount was deducted from his paycheck. It was refunded. For three days before the parade the local Red Cross committee had been after Perez for him to make a contribution.[60]

Because it was alleged that Henry Lattell, 56 years old, of Hoboken, New Jersey, said, "To hell with Liberty bonds, I won't buy any," the man, described as a "registered German alien," was beaten up. As a result, Lattell was in Sgt. Mary's Hospital suffering from a battered head and was in critical condition. Joseph McDonald, 43 years old and from Hoboken, declared he overheard Lattell make that statement. McDonald explained that he demanded that Lattell retract his comments, and when he refused to do so, McDonald hit him and didn't let up until his victim was badly beaten. McDonald was then held on a charge of assault and battery.[61]

John Brankhurst was a 52-year-old night watchman in Los Angeles who was held in the city jail there on June 18, 1918, on charges of, said a news account, "shooting down an American flag, making seditious utterances and being a thrift stamp and liberty loan slacker." The flag was shot down in the office of the Merchants Fire Dispatch, where Brankhurst was employed. The man admitted to shooting down the flag but declared it was an accident.[62]

George McCormick, a boilermaker at the South Pacific Railroad in Sacramento, was reportedly chased around the shop yard by "a hundred other employees who did all but drown McCormick with a fire hose and them camouflaged him with a big bucket of red paint." McCormick refused to buy thrift stamps while the men who chased him had all signed up "for the limit their purses would permit." According to D. S. Watkins, superintendent of the shop, the buying of War Savings Stamps by the Southern Pacific employees had been proceeding until then "on a 100 per cent basis."[63]

A shooting occurred in Morenci, Arizona, which proved to be a mystery to the authorities. Morenci was a company town owned by one of the largest copper mining companies in the world. Deputy McCarty discovered a Mexican suffering from a pistol wound in June 1918, but the wounded man could not be persuaded to say anything about what happened. He maintained that he did not know who shot him or why. It was not a serious wound, and the unnamed man was taken to the hospital, where he recovered. Eventually, the mystery was cleared up when another Mexican man came in and surrendered to Deputy McCarty, acknowledging he shot the other man. Neither man was named in the news stories. The shooter said the incident resulted from a quarrel between the two men over the purchase of thrift stamps. He said he told the victim that he had bought thrift stamps with all the money he had. The victim replied he was a fool to have done so because thrift stamps were worthless, and then the victim proceeded "to abuse the government." That led to heated words, and when the "slacker Mexican" tried to draw his knife, the shooter pulled out his gun and shot the victim. Becoming alarmed, he fled, only to return later to confess. Several witnesses were said to have come forward and corroborated the story. Sheriff Slaughter explained that the shooter would not be prosecuted as the incident was "self-defense,' but "the wounded Mexican will be held for the Federal authorities as soon as he is sufficiently recovered."[64]

Percy Fineout worked at a Wheeler, Oregon lumber mill and found himself in trouble because he allegedly refused to buy or pledge himself to buy War Savings Stamps. Not only did he refuse to purchase the stamps, but he was also said to have disparaged the American government and its system. It was also said he failed to buy Liberty bonds, although he was making a daily wage of $6. One evening as the 200 workmen were leaving the mill yard, Fineout was again approached by a solicitor for the War Savings Stamps campaign. When he refused to buy or pledge himself, yet again, he was seized by some of his fellow workers, and the group started for the waterfront, where he was promised to be given a chance to "imitate a Hun submarine." That forced march toward the waterfront convinced Fineout that he wanted to buy War Savings Stamps and lots of them. The mob then marched to the post office building in Wheeler, where a war stamp was bought for every thousand feet of spruce lumber cut that day at the mill by Fineout. The purchaser also pledged allegiance to the American flag and roundly cursed the Kaiser and his satellites. The article ended with the journalist concluding, "this community is not in a mood to listen to the slurs of any pro-Hun or I. W. W. sympathizer or to condone disloyal or unpatriotic acts of any nature."[65]

Letters were mailed one morning in July 1918 to War Savings Stamps slackers in Ogden, Utah, who had not bought stamps or signed pledges to do so, "telling them in positive terms that it is their duty and obligation to aid." Those letters were sent by the local committee in charge of selling those items. Committee chairman Frank Driggs said that already the efforts of the committee working with those slackers were bearing fruit because the headquarters of the Weber County group had already been visited by "several" slackers who had received letters, "and each was profuse with explanations and reasons why his name had not been attached to a pledge card." The campaign by the committee, declared Driggs, would be continued until all slackers had been rounded up and had either been converted and listed as purchasers or had given "strong" reasons to support their claims to being granted an exemption from the purchasing requirement.[66]

Displayed in the Post Office in Keokuk, Iowa, was a notice about War Savings Stamps, and it contained a stark warning that people must hold those financial instruments and not cash them in. "Are you a war savings stamps slacker? It is an act bordering on treachery to cash stamps when you can afford to hold them. When you bought your war savings stamps you loaned your money to the government to help maintain the soldiers 'over there,'" stated the notice. "The government accepted it in good faith for that purpose. Don't betray our soldiers by asking for money that's being used to clothe, feed and arm them. Keep your war savings stamps. Don't cash them now."[67]

Because Charles Marshall, a puddler at a steel mill in Fort Wayne, Indiana, refused to purchase Liberty bonds, although earning high wages, fellow employees at the plant went on strike on the morning of September 27, 1918, and refused to work with him. According to the news story, "The management took summary action to relieve the patriotic employees, who had been enthusiastic bond buyers, of their embarrassment and Marshall needs a new job."[68]

Henry E. Boatman, W. H. Criss Jr., and Harrison Wheaton were three alleged Liberty Loan slackers of Pierson Township in Indiana. There were, according to press reports, "arraigned before a special investigating committee at the post office building..." After that "trial," the men were sent back to their farms on "probation" after promising to buy bonds of the Fourth Liberty Loan issue, then just starting, and also promising to assist in the campaign in their section of the county. The men had been served with summonses on a Thursday and Friday morning and appeared later on the Friday before a special committee for investigating bond slackers. That committee was composed of Earl Houck of the Vigo County Council of Defense, James S. Royse Jr., R. Hunter, "and a representative of the bureau of investigation of the department of justice." The evidence against the men was not made public, but Royse said that the men "had agreed to conduct themselves in the future so as to set right the opinion that had been formed of them and make themselves to be viewed in a different light in the community in which they lived."[69]

Action was taken on September 28, 1918, by the Rock Island County branch of the National Council of Defense when the local body created a Liberty Loan "court" that would act in all cases where persons failed or refused to subscribe for their "proper share" of Liberty bonds during the Fourth Liberty Loan issue and drive. That so-called court was composed of 16 members and planned to convene each day until the Fourth Liberty Loan drive was over, a period of about 30 days. All people living in Rock Island and the lower part of the county "who fail through a lack of patriotism to purchase their fair share of bonds will be notified to appear before the court and explain why they do not support the loan according to their means." That local Council of Defense requested that all citizens who might learn of a slacker report that case to the Liberty Loan Court.[70]

At the same time, in Scott County, Iowa, every resident of the territory outside of the old city limits of Davenport, Iowa in Scott County had been mailed an official summons from the Scott County Liberty Loan Campaign Committee to present themselves at the registration place in their respective townships between 8:00 AM and 9:00 PM on September 28 "and purchase their full quota of bonds" in the Fourth Liberty Loan drive. The summons mailed out in Scott County read, in part, "This request is made by direction of the United States government in this federal reserve district." And, it continued, "Our government has just completed the registration of all men from 18 to 45, with no exemption to any one, and they are all subject to the draft. Now, the call is made for each of us to loan our money to the government at a fair rate of interest – each his full share, with no exemptions. Both are war measures necessary to save the nation. Do not allow anything to prevent you from responding to this summons."[71]

John Hartzog was a rancher who lived near Brogan, Oregon. Late in September 1918, he found himself to be the "guest" at a "patriotic" Liberty bond party staged in Brogan on a Friday night. According to a report, "He came to the party on a special invitation extended by a group of citizens who called at his home after he had gone to bed." He was solicited that Friday afternoon by a committee of Brogan citizens during a Liberty bond drive. However, he refused to discuss buying bonds until one of their numbers suggested that if he continued to act in that fashion, his motives might be misconstrued. That annoyed Hartzog and prompted him to reply,

"Do you think I am pro-German?" To which a committee member retorted, "We will have to draw our own conclusions for we know you can afford to buy bonds." Hartzog then adamantly refused to buy any bonds, saying, "I don't know that we have a government. I don't know that the bonds of the United States are worth anything any how." The committee then left him, but when the people about town learned of the incident during the remainder of the day, "they determined to bring Hartzog to an accounting." A party was soon formed, which made its way to Hartzog's house, where they found him in bed. They took him from his bed and his house and marched him toward Brogan. By the time the group reached the town, Hartzog had begun to repent and was willing, when Brogan was reached, to subscribe for bonds, but the mob would not agree. Some in the mob wanted to tar and feather him, but other voices prevailed, and the mob contented itself with telling him what they thought of him and also of their determination to turn him over to the county authorities for further action. Sheriff Brown was contacted and instructed the Brogan men to bring Hartzog to Vale, Oregon, the next day. That following day, Hartzog purchased a $100 bond after a little "persuasion" by the sheriff. He also promised to be good in the future, and the matter was dropped there. J. A. Kennedy and Tom Logan of the local Brogan committee reported that people had long been "incensed" at Hartzog's attitude, "which has been anything but loyal." Reportedly, he had never taken out a membership in the Red Cross, for example. Said Kennedy; "The people up there have decided that such things will not be tolerated in our community and since Hartzog has been one of the most prominent offenders it was time that an example was set. If there are any more like him in the district, they will get the same treatment."[72]

According to Charles H. Davis of the Lansing Chamber of Commerce, a Liberty Loan "draft board" was set up in Lansing, Michigan, and reportedly was having no trouble selling its quota of bonds, according to Charles H. Davis of the Lansing Chamber of Commerce. Said Davis; "We only draft slackers. We do not get after them until the volunteers have done their share. We start by making a census through gas and electric company records and those of employers, whether one man or a thousand. In this way, we get a line on who ought to buy bonds and about how much they should be able to take." Then the group set two days aside for the "volunteers." Everyone in Lansing was expected to sign their "volunteer card," which was a subscription blank to buy bonds. Those forms went through a sort of clearinghouse where they were checked off against the group's census list. Davis explained, "Up to this point, it has been all 'volunteer' subscribing. We have kept away from imperative commands to 'buy' or 'lend.'" After checking the census was done, the group called in people who had oversubscribed, who had been "overly "patriotic" in taking more than they could handle. Unless one of those identified told the group they had more income than the group's records indicated. For those who had genuinely oversubscribed, the group "cut down their subscriptions and make the slackers carry the surplus." When the slackers were called before the group, the first thing that happened was that reasons were demanded from them to explain their failure to subscribe. If a good reason was offered; for example, a man with a sick wife and high medical expenses the committee knew nothing about, then he was "exempted" and was given a subscriber's badge so he would not feel humiliated when he met his neighbors as he went about his life. Davis then stated, with respect to the "real" delinquents, "The rest we 'draft' into the loan." However, Davis provided no specific details.[73]

The Crown Willamette Paper Company was located in West Linn, Oregon, a community now part of greater Portland. The firm's flag pole was requisitioned one Monday afternoon when a man by the name of P. C. Sonnasyn, a "self-confessed" bond slacker, was, according to reports, "given the ride of his life by a bunch of husky mill workers who first treated the slacker's back to a broad stripe of yellow paint. Sonnasyn lived on a farm near West Linn and worked at the mill on a part-time basis during his farm's slack season. Reportedly he had sold $2,000 worth of wheat recently but told bond solicitors that the United States meant nothing to him, a remark that earned him a free ride on the "Liberty pole," which was 15 feet long, painted red, white, and blue with handles at each end and the word "liberty" inscribed upon it. On that Monday afternoon, Sonnasyn was seized by fellow employees at the plant, painted yellow, placed on the pole, and carried for some distance. At this point, he begged to be let off and promised to subscribe to a bond which he did. It was also said that Sonnasyn declined to subscribe to the latest Red Cross drive until a threshing crew refused to come to his farm to thresh his grain until he donated $5 to the Red Cross campaign. His wife had recently secured a divorce from him. At the same time, in nearby Oregon City, Oregon, it was reported that Julius Krasnewski, an employee of the Hawley Pulp and Paper Company, was no longer with the firm. He would have been fired the following Monday if he had shown up for work, but he had fled the area by then. On Saturday night, his fellow employees treated him to a cold water bath following his refusal to purchase a Liberty bond, and Krasnewski quickly left town for parts unknown.[74]

In Redding, California, a group of 150 people who could afford to buy bonds but had not and a group of 27 people who had not bought as many as they could afford were given, on October 7, 1918, until October 19 "to prove that they are Americans." If they had not satisfied the Redding local bond committee at that time, they were to be turned over to a committee of five "conservative business men." That committee would hear excuses, and if they were satisfied by the offered reasons, that man's name would be dropped from the list. If the committee was not satisfied with the excuses offered, then it planned to publish the names of those men in black type as the "roll of dishonor" and would report them to the California Council of Defense and the federal authorities for further action.[75]

While the action of the so-called "Knights of Liberty" in parading through the streets of Tulsa, Oklahoma, warning Liberty Loan slackers, was not countermanded by the Liberty Loan organization, it nevertheless declared the Knights to be out of sympathy with the policies of the Liberty committee. A statement made by J. M. Berry, chairman of the Tulsa County Liberty Loan organization, asserted, "We do not need to coerce any one, in order to go over the top with our quota. Any man who is not loyal enough to back up our army in France with his money is a slacker, but we will not force him, through fear of bodily harm, into doing that which his patriotism should permit him to do." Added Berry, "I want everyone to know and understand that the action of the band of masked men Friday night was without the knowledge or sanction of our committee. We will sell our full quota of bonds in Tulsa, but we will not resort to physical force in order to do it."[76]

Amid the Fourth Liberty Loan campaign in October 1918, an article outlining that drive appeared in a Harrisburg, Pennsylvania, newspaper. One theme of that campaign was for subscribers to buy twice as many bonds as they did during the Third Loan drive. That article began by declaring, "The one outstanding feature of today at Liberty Loan headquarters was the extraordinarily large number of reports of 'bond slackers' and the increasing large number of complaints from bond owners who declare that while they do not object to 'doubling the third' they think it absolutely ridiculous they 'double the third' while thousands of Harrisburg men and women have not bought bonds at all." One example given was of an unnamed "high-salaried" tradesman who bought no bonds and explained he did not do so because US President Woodrow Wilson "got us into a war we had no business in." A second example was a family that resided on Green Street. They had six wage and salary earners but still purchased no bonds. According to the article, a wage-earner went to Liberty Loan headquarters and stated: "I think it is an outrage that something is not done to make all the people of Harrisburg hold up their end of this war. I earn about $30 a week. I have a total of $700 worth of bonds in all the loans, not all of them paid for yet. I think I am holding up my end. But when I hear of prominent people who are buying $2,500 worth of bonds, and men making fine salaries who aren't buying any bonds, and farmers who haven't bought a bond in all four issues, but charge 65 cents a dozen for eggs, then I get boiling mad." Liberty Loan committee secretary Clyde Myton reportedly had a "long list" of bond slackers, their addresses and occupations that had been "furnished him by amateur sleuths..." Banks in Harrisburg were to be asked for complete details of bond subscriptions, but it was acknowledged that the banks might "not come through" with that information.[77]

An editorial in the same issue as the above article continued to discuss the issue of slackers. According to the editor, there were two types of slackers. One type was the man of limited means who bought one bond when "down in his heart he knows he could pay on the installment plan for two or three." The second type of slacker was the man who had the money but held back to find investments that paid a higher rate of return, such as six or seven percent. "One is as bad as the other. Both are yellow to the core. Neither one is fit to be called an American. Both ought to be held up to the public as examples of bad citizenship," declared the editor. In conclusion, the newspaper man fumed, "They are the half-hearted, yellow-streaked men who place their fat purses before their country and therefore, in reality, have no country. They are the creatures whom the poet said 'go down to the vile dust from which they sprung, unwept, unhonored and unsung."[78]

The headline from an article in a Texas newspaper discussing the situation in Arizona observed that people in that state were "rough" with loan slackers. In Mesa, Arizona, a "substantial farmer" of the area claimed his religion would not permit him in any way to aid the war effort and withstood all community efforts to change his mind. As a result, an effigy of the man was hung in one of the city's main streets. In Hayden, Arizona, a man of Danish birth was said to have made "unpatriotic remarks" concerning the Liberty Loan posters. A posse took him to the city limits and gave him a coat of tar and feathers. He was rescued by the police and given comparative safety in jail, from which refuge he was sent out of town the next morning. Also noted in the article was that in each of the communities, there were published lists of bond subscribers "and later there may be lists of non-subscribers."[79]

"With this exception, we are 100 percent," read the sign displayed on the chest of Charles Reas, a carpenter in the employ of the Arizona Eastern Railroad company in Phoenix, Arizona. That sign referred to the fact that Reas had bought no bonds. A mob, made up of his fellow employees, seized him, tied his hands in front of it, hung the sign on his chest, placed a rope around his neck, and led him on a march through the business streets of Phoenix on the evening of October 15, 1918. In addition, the procession included automobiles, with other men and boys from the area joining the parade as it passed, with much shouting and jeering. The employees of Arizona Eastern in Phoenix had all purchased bonds in the earlier Third Liberty Loan and were determined to equal that figure in the Fourth Liberty Loan, but Reas was a stumbling block standing in the way of that goal being attained. Reas turned a deaf ear to all pleas and entreaties to subscribe to bonds. Then it was decided to make an object lesson of him. At quitting time at the railroad yard on October 15, they told Reas what they intended to do. At first, he paid no attention, but when he saw they meant business, he had a change of heart and offered to buy a bond. But it was too late, and his coworkers carried out their intentions. Procuring yellow paint, they painted his face and hat, hung the sign on him, and trussed him up in preparation for the procession. When the parade reached the corner of Washington and Central, Reas was made to bow to the Statute of Liberty and kiss the flag. As the procession continued, it got bigger, and the jeering increased. The police were reported to be keeping a sharp eye on the proceedings, fearing the breakout of violence. At Second Avenue and the railroad tracks, the police took charge of the man and escorted him to the police station, where he was kept for protection. Later he was released. The Liberty Loan Committee, however, learning of the situation, ordered Reas to be again taken into custody, and police officer Broyles, at a late hour on Friday night, arrested Reas and took him to the police station. A search of his clothing revealed that he had $223.97 in cash on his person. Reas, who said he was born in St. Paul and was an American, a single man with no dependents, and "thus his refusal to buy a bond is considered to be absolutely without excuse." He had been in the employ of Arizona Eastern for about two years.[80]

A couple of days later, Reas, after being rescued and released by the police, was taken before the local Liberty Loan Committee to explain why he had not bought any bonds. Reas then bought a $100 bond and told them he had been in an insane asylum on the coast, and since being released from that institution, he was suspicious of all investments. He added that when he went into the asylum, he had considerable property and that while in the asylum, supposed friends succeeded in getting all his property from him so that when he was released, he was destitute. According to this account, at the time the police intervened, the group had become a "mob," and threats were made on the life of Reas, and that clubs, rocks, and other weapons were in evidence. Reas spent that night in jail, contradicting the earlier account that the police took him into custody twice on the same day.[81]

On October 22, Reas was committed to the state hospital for the insane in Arizona by order of Judge R. C. Stanford of the Maricopa County Superior Court. Discovered by a motorist, Reas was wandering aimlessly on the Yuma road nine miles from Phoenix. Reas was brought to town by the motorist and turned over to the police. During his occasional semi-rational moments, Reas told that motorist that he had been without food for three days and had been fired upon several times as he wandered around. He also said that the mob in Phoenix tried to hang him there. When searched at the police station, he was found to have a check for $90.99, a railroad ticket to Los Angeles, "and other articles of value." After an examination at the police station by Dr. A. B. Nichols, county physician, Reas was declared insane, a commitment order was signed by Stanford, and he was at once taken to the state hospital east of Phoenix. Dr. Nichols declared that Reas had been insane for some time but that he did not hold the recent treatment of him at the hands of a mob as responsible for his current condition. That pronouncement by Nichols allowed the police to declare that an investigation or arrest of mob members was unnecessary. Thus they dropped the matter.[82]

Not everyone wanted the matter dropped. An editorial in a Phoenix newspaper said, "There should be a full investigation of the outrage committed on the man, Charles Reas, in the name of patriotism the other day." The editor pointed out there was then a controversy over whether he was insane before he was mobbed or whether the mob treatment drove him insane, but the editor could not understand why that should be a factor in having or not having a police investigation. Nevertheless, nothing more was ever heard or written about Charles Reas.[83]

Fear that he was about to receive rough treatment at the hands of his fellow employees at the Daniels Construction Company plant in Marin County, California, caused Mike Benich to send out a call for help to Sheriff Keating. Two officers responded and took Benich into custody for questioning. When he was queried, Benich admitted the trouble at the quarry was caused by his refusal to buy Liberty bonds when he was financially able to do so. He said he had cash and bank deposits that totaled $1,466. Benich was described as a 52-year-old Austrian who had been in America for 12 years. He had three brothers serving in the Austrian army. According to the news account, "The man finally was persuaded that an investment with Uncle Sam was perfectly safe, and he bought $450 worth of Liberty Bonds."[84]

"Every Liberty Loan slacker in McMechen [WV] will buy a bond during the present campaign or else," was the threatening statement made on an October 1918 evening by a member of the "Strong Arm Committee" of the McMechen Liberty Loan organization. Added the spokesman; "Furthermore every person who is not showing his Liberty Bond honor flag or button, and whose name is not on the honor rolls will be dealt with severely."[85]

That same month Fayette County, Kentucky, was reportedly going after its bond slackers with methods that were "bound to attract attention," remarked a journalist. A Bourbon County, Kentucky man who had been to Fayette County on an inspection tour of the tobacco crop told a newsman that he saw "hundreds" of placards in different parts of the county, worded as follows: "Notice to the Public. This is to notify the people of Fayette county that _____, a wealthy and prominent citizen, is a Liberty Loan slacker, and as such, should be shunned by the people of this county and the State." The man named in the placard was described as a wealthy farmer residing on a "handsome estate" near the Bourbon and Fayette line. According to the news account, "What effect this publicity and notoriety will have on his purse strings remains to be seen. But it ought to be effective, to say the least."[86]

In a mass meeting for Liberty bonds, a large crowd of several hundred people gathered one evening in Baxter Springs, Kansas and wrote a reporter, "they heard a quantity of forceful language directed against the persons who have refused to buy bonds in proportion to their means." Said one speaker, the Reverend John Garretson, "If it is right for the government to enter the homes and take the young men away to war, it is also right for the government to enter the banks and conscript the surplus money that fortunate individuals have piled up, and now refuse to loan to the government in this time of need." His remarks were reported to have been "warmly applauded."[87]

John M. Cordoza described as an "alien," was installed in the county jail at Santa Cruz, California, for 90 days, having been brought up from Watsonville, California, where he was sentenced to the jail term for his "defiant attitude" toward the Liberty Loan committee and the United States government. Although he had sufficient funds to buy bonds, he refused to buy any Liberty bonds.[88]

"One by one the men who have refused to and are refusing to buy Liberty Bonds are being found out," wrote a reporter in Farmington, Missouri. He added, "The weight of public opinion is striking at the individual who can buy and who doesn't. It is striking just as hard at the man or the woman of property who buys a little $50 bond when that subscription ought to be multiplied. For the people know, the neighbors accurately gauge, just about what each of us should be able to do."[89]

In Pennsylvania, the Lehigh County Liberty Loan Committee printed the names of nearly 100 Austrian employees of Northampton Industries who refused to subscribe to Liberty bonds. Those men were described as Austrians, although nothing was said about their citizenship status in America. As a result of that activity, all of them were discharged by the company, and a blacklist was established under which other industries in the area were asked not to employ them.[90]

Because he refused to buy Liberty bonds and made "seditious remarks," A. C. Maas of Clipper Gap, California, was fined by Justice of the Peace Seaton. After he was fined, Maas gave $100 to the Red Cross, $100 to the Y. M. C. A., and he also agreed to buy $300 of War Savings Stamps.[91]

Bernard Petrasko, 18 years old, was killed, and Paul Dunn and George Worms were seriously wounded during a riot that occurred on Saturday night, October 19, 1918, in front of the business establishment of Charles Fischer, a German baker at McKees Rocks, Pennsylvania, who became enraged when a mob entered his shop and demanded that he purchase a Liberty bond. That action by the mob prompted Fischer to open fire with a revolver into the crowd. "Lynch him" and "Down with the pro-German" were cries sent up by the crowd following the shooting. Police prevented further violence by taking Fischer out of his store through a back window to the county jail. Fischer was charged with manslaughter. According to the police Fischer, who last spring was severely beaten by a mob as a result of his "pro-German tendencies" during a Red Cross campaign, refused to buy a bond when approached by the district Liberty Loan Committee and made "insulting remarks" about the government. The news of the refusal spread, and a crowd assembled in front of the bakery shouting, "Buy a bond!" The shooting followed shortly after that. This story was picked up, in briefer form, by a few newspapers at the time it happened. However, there was no follow-up anywhere after October. That was very unusual considering the gravity of the case, and it led one to believe that it may not have happened at all.[92]

E. W. Thompson of Brookfield Township, Pennsylvania initiated a suit in the local courts late in October 1918 to recover $25,000 damages against nine residents of Brookfield Township – several of them being police and bank officials – charging that "they injured his pride, bruised his shins and shattered his health by exposing him to the night air a few nights earlier when they dragged him from his home because he refused to buy a Liberty Bond." In his statement, Thompson declared he was willing to buy a bond, but his visitors became abusive, and he ordered them out of his house. Then they "roughly handled him and placed handcuffs on his wrists, after which he was thrown carelessly into a buggy." During that ordeal, Thompson declared that his shins were skinned, and he was subjected to the jeers of a large crowd that had gathered to watch the proceedings. Besides his pride being injured, he declared that exposure to the night air made him ill.[93]

Henry Bleick and Joseph Graml were residents of Fairfax, Minnesota. According to a local newspaper Bleick had been allotted $800 in Liberty bonds as the amount he should purchase, while Graml was marked down for $350. Each of them refused to buy the amount dictated as their share or to buy any bonds at all. After refusing to subscribe, they were advised by chairman T. O'Connor of the Safety Commission to appear before that body to explain themselves. They failed to appear on October 25, 1918, and a summons was issued to each with a command to appear before the agency on October 29. Once again, each failed to appear, and a bench warrant was issued, and they were separately arrested for contempt of court. Sheriff Slade brought them to Olivia, Minnesota, and as soon as the sheriff reached Olivia with the two prisoners, a crowd gathered and got the prisoners away from the authorities. The mob made the slackers kneel and kiss the American flag. Then the mob marched the pair to jail, forcing each one to carry high above his head an American flag. The following day, the men appeared before Judge Daly at Renville, Minnesota, where "an adjustment of the matter" was made. Bleick subscribed for $1,500 worth of bonds, donated $100 to the Red Cross, donated $100 to the War Work

Fund, and paid $109.54 in fines and court costs." Graml subscribed for $750 worth of bonds, donated $75 to the Red Cross, donated $50 to the War Work Fund, and paid fines and court costs of $109.54.[94]

As a result of alleged malicious rioting and trespass in connection with the Fourth and Fifth Liberty Loan campaigns in Carroll County, Indiana, bench warrants were issued in the Carroll County Circuit Court in June 1919 for the arrest of several "of the more prominent citizens" of the county. The warrants were the outgrowth of the alleged activities of the accused in attempts to get a number of Dunkards to buy bonds. [Dunkards were a group of German-American Baptists opposed to military service]. These farmers said they opposed war and would not buy bonds to support it. Among those with outstanding arrest warrants were: John U. Shanks, president of the Bank of Camden (Indiana); Arthur Ritchey, a manufacturer; Fred George, Edward Cripe, and Gill Patty, all of whom were local politicians. It was alleged that the home of Daniel Miller, who had not purchased bonds, was visited at midnight by an automobile party. Miller said he was called from bed, threatened with violence, windows in his home were broken, and paint smeared on the house. The men are alleged to have told Miller he had a few days in which to buy bonds. He took out a subscription the next day.[95]

Seven members of the Emmet County, Iowa War Board were sued in October 1920 for $40,000 by the Lee brothers, who lived just north of Estherville, Iowa, the county seat of Emmet County. They charged that the war board caused a yellow billboard to be constructed and erected in the public square of Estherville, carrying the names of the Lee brothers in large black type as bond slackers. The war board consisted of 13 members, six of whom were omitted from the lawsuit, but it was reported those six had joined with the others "of their own accord, and will appear as co-defendants." That war board often adjusted the assessments made by the township boards for Liberty bond subscriptions during the war. However, in the case of the Lee brothers, during the Fourth Liberty Loan drive, the board upheld the assessment for the Lee brothers. When the Lee brothers refused to accept the quota for bond purchases assigned to them, the billboard was painted yellow, and the names of the Lee brothers were printed on it. The sign was then carried around the streets of Estherville in a parade. The suit was for damages sustained in those acts. Each plaintiff sought judgment for $10,000 in actual damages and $100,000 in exemplary damages.[96]

An editorial on the above lawsuit, which appeared in an Iowa newspaper, was furious. The editor thought there was little chance of success and declared, "People are more kinds of a fool than there are classifications who at this late date desire to stir up their own shortcomings in our liberty bond drives. If they are not content to keep still in an effort to live down their disgrace they had better sell out and move away to a new start somewhere."[97]

A verdict in the Lee case was delivered in February 1921, and, as expected, it went against the Lee brothers and in favor of the Emmet County War Board. Reportedly, war mothers and American Legion members joyfully paraded on the streets of Estherville after the verdict against wealthy farmer C. O. Lee and his brother was delivered by the jury; that jury deliberated for two hours."[98]

Notes.

Chapter 1.

1.   Richard   Sutch.   "Liberty   bonds."
www.federalreservehistory.org/essays/Liberty_bonds[1].
Accessed Aug 18 2019.

2. Ibid.

3. Ibid.

4. Ibid.

5. Ibid.

6. Ibid.

7.   "Liberty   bonds."   https://en.wikipedia.org/wiki/
Liberty_bond. Accessed Aug 19 2019.

8. Ibid.

9. "A bond slacker would be the cheapest slacker on earth."
Evening Times-Republican (Marshalltown

IA), Apr 24 1919.

10. "Banks plan cash for district in big loan drive." *Harrisburg Telegraph* (PA), Oct 1 1918; Ad.

Public Ledger (Maysville KY), Oct 2 1918.

11. "Urge slackers to buy bonds." *El Paso Herald* (TX), June 9 1917.

12. "The slacker." *De Soto County News* (Arcadia FL), Apr 20 1916.

13. "Loan quotas fixed." *Evening Public Ledger* (Philadelphia), Apr 5 1918; "$4,170,019,650 is total

reached by liberty loan." *Washington Times*, May 18 1918.

14. "Bond investors increase because of liberty bonds. *Record* (Greenville KY), Apr 18 1918.

15. "War Savings Stamps of the United States." wikipedia.org, accessed Aug 19 2019.

16. "Liberty loan slackers." *Grand Forks Herald* (ND), Apr 29 1918.

17. "Financial news and comment." *Sun* (NY), May 19, 1917.

18. James Corbett. "War profiteering in WW1." www.sgtreport.com/2018/12/war-profiteering-in-WW1[2]

accessed Aug 19 2019.

19. Ibid.

20. "Makes another expose of profits." *Butte Bulletin* (MT), Jul 5 1920.

21. "Trade board exposes war profits." *Labor World* (Duluth MN), May 29 1920.

22. "Sen. Capper scores the profiteers." *Grand Forks Herald* (ND), Apr 24, 1920.

23. "What profiteers made." *Labor World* (Duluth MN), Sep 16 1922.

24. "Many bad bills slated to pass after election" *Labor World* (Duluth MN), Oct 7 1922.

25. "War debt in billions." *Tomahawk* (White Earth MN), Apr 18 1918.

26. "Financial cost of the First World War." www.spartacus-educational.com[3], accessed Aug 17 2019.

27. "Summary of receipts, outlays and surpluses or deficits 1789-2021."

www.obamawhitehouse.archives.gov/omb/budget/historicals[4], accessed Aug 17 2019.

28. "Uncle Sam's ability to pay war bonds is eleven times Great Britain's, figures show."

Detroit Times, Oct 4 1917.

---

29. Chase Peterson-Withorn. "From Rockefeller to Ford, see Forbes' 1918 ranking of the richest

people in America." www.forbes.com[5], accessed Aug 22 2019.

30. "Statistical statement of deposits in the United States. www.chestofbooks.com/finance/banking[6],

accessed Aug 20 2019.

Chapter 2.

1. "Liberty bond slackers put on the grill." *Evening Public Ledger* (Philadelphia), Jun 4 1917.

2. Ibid.

3. "Bond slackers' last chance." *Evening Public Ledger* (Philadelphia), Jun 5 1917.

4. Ad. *Sun* (NY), Jun 7 1917.

5. "Urge slackers to buy bonds." *El Paso Herald* (TX), Jun 9 1917.

6. "Chickasha bond slackers will be rounded up by ten committees now on job." *Chickasha Express*

(OK), June 13 1917; "Express packagettes." *Chickasha Express*, Jun 14 1917.

7. "Huge issue taken by over 2,000,000." *Evening World* (NY), Jun 15 1917.

8. "Paying a dollar a week for war." *New York Tribune*, Jul 30 1917.

9. "Avoid slow starting of liberty bond drive." *Barre Times* (VT), Oct 2 1917.

10. "War bonds sell fast already." *Detroit Times*, Oct 4 1917.

11. Ad. *Williston Graphic* (ND), Oct 11 1917.

12. "Road to ask 160,000 to take loan bond." *Washington Herald*, Oct 12 1917.

---

5.   http://www.forbes.com/

6.   http://www.chestofbooks.com/finance/banking

13. "No slack in drive for liberty loan" *Evening Star* (Washington), Oct 12 1917.

14. "Campaign starts out well; women to do their bit." *Grand Forks Herald* (ND), Oct 15 1917.

15. "First billion dollars have been subscribed." *Grand Forks Herald* (ND), Oct 16 1917; "Motor king

himself buys $5,000,000; remainder for employees." *Detroit Times*, Oct 16 1917.

16. "Shaw reached to hip pocket says worker." *Oklahoma City Times*, Oct 18 1917.

17. "Shameful says Shaw's rich brother." *Oklahoma City Times*, Oct 18 1917.

18. Ad. *Evening Times-Republican* (Marshalltown IA), Oct 20 1917.

19. Ad. *Oklahoma City Times*, Oct 20 1917.

20. "Buy a bond." *Wheeling Intelligencer* (WV), Oct 19 1917.

21. "Sales of bonds more than two and half million here." *Oklahoma City Times*, Oct 20 1917.

22. "Are you a liberty loan slacker?" *West Virginian* (Fairmont), Oct 20 1917.

23. "Bond slackers to be hunted down." *Tulsa World*, Oct 21 1917.

24. Ad. *Bennington Evening Banner* (VT), Oct 23 1917.

25. Ibid.

26. "Safety gates in the hear of Philadelphia." *Evening Public Ledger* (Philadelphia), Oct 24 1917.

27. "Pro-Germans under probe." *Evening Star* (Washington), Oct 30 1917.

28. "Stamp slackers called mutts by Billy Sunday." *Washington Times*, Jan 23 1918.

29. Ad. *Washington Times*, Jan 23 1918.

30. "Just you." *Aberdeen Weekly* (MS), Feb 22 1918.

31. Ad. *Chickasha Express* (OK), Feb 27 1918.

32. "Liberty bond slackers found by credit men." *Evening Public Ledger* (Philadelphia), Mar 15 1918.

33. "Liberty loan slackers will have no way to escape from local canvassing committee."

Ogden Standard (UT), Apr 10 1918.

34. "City far from quota set for bond campaign." *Oklahoma City Times*, Apr 10 1918.

35. "Too many holding back on war loan." *Seattle Star*, Apr 18 1918.

36. Ad. *Coconino Sun* (Flagstaff AZ), Apr 19, 1918.

37. "Spotlight for loan slackers." *Seattle Star*, Apr 19 1918.

38. "Loan slackers are to be given much publicity." *Ogden Standard* (UT), Apr 25 1918.

39. "40,000 will march in big bond parade." *Washington Herald*, Apr 25 1918; "Friday, April 26

Liberty Day by proclamation." *New Mexico State Record* (Santa Fe), Apr 26 1918.

40. Ad. *Banner* (Cambridge MD), Apr 26 1918.

41. "Bridgeport is first in district to get quota." *Bridgeport Times and Evening Farmer* (CT),

Apr 26 1918.

42. "Four-minute men to appear in all the theaters." *Ogden Standard* (UT), Apr 26 1918.

43. "Buy liberty bonds." *New Iberia Enterprise* (LA), Apr 27 1918.

44. "Liberty loan slackers should avoid these maids." *Evening Public Ledger* (Philadelphia),

Apr 27 1918.

45. "He who subscribes nothing to defense not entitled to it" *Evening Herald* (Albuquerque NM),

May 1 1918.

46. "Soldier puts bond up to folks behind." *Evening Star* (Washington), May 1 1918.

47. William Hamilton Osborne. "I haven't got the money, weakest of all excuses for Liberty bond
slacker." *Evening World* (NY), May 1 1918.

48. "Seek bond slackers." *Manitowoc Pilot* (WI), May 2 1918.

49. "Thrift stamp campaign speeded up again." *Evening Public Ledger* (Philadelphia), May 7 1918.

50. Ad. *Alaska Empire* (Juneau), May 8 1918.

51. "State defense council after bond slackers." *Clearwater Republican* (ID), May 10 1918.

52. Ad. *Orleans County Monitor* (Barton VT), Jun 19 1918.

53. "May make list of thrift stamp slackers." *Chattanooga News* (TN), June 11 1918.

54. Two bit bards give thrift stamps fame." *Sun* (NY), June 23 1918.

55. "Oregon quota for 4th loan decided upon." *Rogue River Courier* (Grant's Pass OR), Jul 10 1918.

56. "Bond slacker question." *Colusa Sun* (CA), August 24 1918.

57. "Bond slackers to be checked in next drive." *Montpelier Examiner* (ID), Aug 30 1918.

58. "People and events." *Omaha Bee*, Sep 2 1918.

59. "The allotment plan." *Little Falls Herald* (MN), Sep 6 1918.

60. "Some Liberty loan slogans." *Camden Chronicle* (TN), Sep 20 1918.

61. "W. S. S. slackers are still evident." *Richmond Palladium* (IN), Sep 23 1918.

62. "Fourth liberty loan train stops here." *Journal-Miner* (Prescott AZ), Sep 25 1918.

63. "Outlines plans for raising next loan." *Journal-Miner* (Prescott AZ), Sep 25 1918.

64. "Slacker committee will round up pro-Germans." *Lynden Tribune* (WA), Sep 25 1918.

65. "$75,000 worth of 4th loan Lynden's share." *Lynden Tribune* (WA), Sep 25 1918.

66. "Vigilance committee to be very alive." *El Paso Herald* (TX), Sep 25 1918.

67. "Lend and put a crimp in bill says Arizona." *El Paso Herald* (TX), Oct 2 1918.

68. "Are there liberty loan slackers in Grand Forks City?" *Grand Forks Herald* (ND), Oct 3 1918.

69. "Put your bond out of temptation's way." Maui News (Wailuku HI), Oct 4 1918.

70. "Keep faith with our crusaders." *Chico Record* (CA), Oct 5 1918.

71. "Loan far behind in this district." *Evening Public Ledger* (Philadelphia), Oct 5 1918.

72. Ad. *Arizona Republican* (Phoenix), Oct 7 1918.

73. "City must buy $100,000 bonds a day to win." *Arizona Republican* (Phoenix), Oct 7 1918.

74. "Shock committee will start after tight was tomorrow." *Arizona Republican* (Phoenix),
Oct 14 1918.

75. "Loan tide turns toward success." *Evening Public Ledger* (Philadelphia), Oct 9 1918.

76. "Raleigh to call roll of the bond slackers." *Hickory Record* (NC), Oct 9 1918.

77. "Man who fails to buy bonds is being found out, marked." *Okolona Messenger* (MS), Oct 17 1918.

78. Ad. *Washington Standard* (Olympia), Oct 18 1918.

79. "Brown has a say." *Grenada Sentinel* (MS), Oct 18 1918.

80. "Four billions of loan subscribed." *Sun* (NY), Oct 18 1918.

81. "Uncle Sam's talking machine has 40,000 voices for war work." *Seattle Star,* Oct 19 1918.

82. "Government to stir up war savings stamps slackers." *Bourbon News* (Paris KY), Dec 27 1918.

83. "Calls Liberty bond sellers slackers." *Washington Times*, May 28 1920.

Chapter 3.

1. "Bank takes $3,000,000 of bonds." *Detroit Times*, Jun 4 1917.

2. "Don't be a slacker." *South Bend News-Times* (IN), Jun 12 1917.

3. "Red Cross slackers." *Harrisburg Telegraph* (PA), Apr 12 1917.

4. "Catholic leader hits Sunday trail." *Washington Times,* Jun 9 1917.

5. "Make dollars hit the trail is plea of Billy Sunday." *Seattle Star*, Oct 22 1917.

6. "Don't be a Red Cross slacker." *Lake County Times* (Hammond IN), Jul 20 1917.

7. "The Red Cross slacker." *Gazette-Times* (Heppner OR), Jul 12 1917.

8. No title. *Herald and News* (Newberry SC), Oct 16 1917.

9. "The worst slacker of all." *Oklahoma City Times*, Oct 17 1917.

10. "Liberty loan the anchor of security." *Wheeling Intelligencer* (WV), Oct 19 1917.

11. "The Liberty loan meeting." *Missoulian* (Missoula MT), Oct 21 1917.

12. No title. *Richmond Times-Dispatch* (VA), Oct 22 1917.

13. "Are you 100 percent American?" *Seattle Star,* Oct 22 1917.

14. "Slackers." *Evening Herald* (Klamath Falls OR), Oct 23 1917.

15. George Ade. The slacker." *Clearwater Republican* (Orofino ID), Oct 26 1917.

16. "The next loan." *Lancaster News* (SC), Mar 29 1918.

17. "The financial slacker." *Plateau Voice* (CO), Apr 12 1918.

18. "A liberty loan prayer." *Hartford Herald* (KY), Apr 3 1918.

19. "Loan drive goes over $40,000,000." *Evening Public Ledger* (Philadelphia), Apr 12 1918.

20. "Shun bond slacker, says United States Senator Smoot." *Logan Republican* (UT), Apr 16 1918.

21. "Pay that debt, says Bill Hart." *Logan Republican* (UT), Apr 16 1918.

22. "Force only to be deciding factor." *Tomahawk* (White Earth MN), Apr 18 1918.

23. Roland G. Usher. "Lend your money to help win war." *Tomahawk* (White Earth MN), Apr 18 1918.

24. "Charlie Chaplin's visit." *Watchman and Southern* (Sumter SC), Apr 20 1918.

25. "Prodding the slacker." *Terre Haute Tribune* (IN), Apr 28 1918.

26. "Assails money slackers." *New York Times*, Apr 29, 1918.

27. "Now for the over-subscriptions." *Oklahoma City Times*, Oct 22, 1917.

28. "Financial slackers." *Carrizozo News* (NM), Apr 19 1918.

29. "Liberty loan slackers." *Grand Forks Herald* (ND), Apr 29 1918.

30. Ibid.

31. "Lead dollar loyalty." *Evening Journal* (Wilmington DE), May 1 1918.

32. "As to bond slackers." *Tonopah Bonanza* (NV), May 8 1918.

33. "Slackers?" *New York Times*, Aug 24 1918.

34. "Cures for bond slacking." *New York Times*, Oct 11 1918.

35. "The fate of the bond slacker." *Sun* (NY), Oct 12 1918.

36. "War exhibit drew crows." *Alma Record* (MI), Oct 17 1918.

37. "Drafting the dollar." *Oklahoma City News,* Oct 17 1917.

38. "Liberty loan slackers." *New York Times,* Oct 13 1917.

39. "Everett True and the Liberty loan slackers." *Grand Forks Herald* (ND), Oct 15 1917.

40. "The voice of the people." *Evening Public Ledger* (Philadelphia), Oct 16 1917.

41. "Liberty loan slackers." *Leavenworth Echo* (WA), Nov 2 1917.

42. No title. *Clearwater Republican* (Orofino ID), Nov 9 1917.

43. "Liberty bond slackers." *Dickinson Press* (ND), Nov 3 1917.

44. "Bond slackers should be sent into trenches." *Omaha Bee*, Apr 13 1918.

45. No title. *Athena Press* (OR), Apr 19, 1918.

46. "Liberty bond slackers." *Bisbee Review* (AZ), Apr 19 1918.

47. "Ostracize slackers." *Columbia Herald* (TN), Apr 19 1918.

48. "The fourth liberty loan." *Robersonian* (Lumberton NC), Oct 3 1918.

49. No title. *Montrose Press* (CO), Oct 11 1918.

50. "Buy bonds or give up U.S. to barbarian." *Chico Record* (CA), Oct 13 1918.

51. "The financial slacker." *Mt. Sterling Advocate* (KY), Oct 15 1918.

Chapter 4.

1. Ad. *Evening World* (NY), Apr 30 1918; Ad. *Wheeling Intelligencer* (WV), Apr 30 1918.

2. Ad. *Greeneville Sun* (TN), Oct 3 1918.

3. Ad. *Evening Star* (Washington), Oct 8 1918.

4. Ad. *Sacramento Union* (CA), Oct 15 1918.

5. Ad. *New York Tribune*, Oct 15 1918.

6. Ad. *Evening World* (NY), Oct 16 1918.

7. Ad. *Arizona Republican* (Phoenix), Oct 17 1918.

8. "Liberty loan fraud brings bankruptcy to club promoter." *Oklahoma City Times*, Nov 16 1917.

9. "Used liberty loan to defraud women and children." *Robesonian* (Lumberton NC), Nov 19 1917.

10. "Dwiggins held by grand jury in loan fraud." *New York Tribune*, Nov 22 1917.

11. "Three years for Dwiggins." *Evening Times-Republican* (Marshalltown IA), Dec 28 1917.

12. "Liberty bond scalpers prey on the needy." *New York Tribune*, Apr 9 1918.

13. Ibid.

14. "Loan committee acts to block bond scalpers." *New York Tribune*, Apr 10 1918.

15. "Straus plans to balk liberty loan sharks." *New York Tribune*, Apr 18 1918.

16. "Loan bond complaint bureau." *Sun* (NY), Sept 21 1918.

17. "Liberty bond scalpers are target of crusade." *Evening World* (NY), Sep 28 1918.

18. "Bond scalpers attacked." *New York Tribune*, Oct 29 1918.

19. "Warns against loan scalpers." *Richmond Palladium* (IN), Apr 5 1919.

20. "You can help get scalpers of bonds." *Camden Chronicle* (TN), Apr 25 1919.

21. "Glass advised of way to curb bond fraud." *New York Tribune*, Apr 17 1919.

22. "McAdoo calls on N.Y. for $1,800,000,000 of 4th loan." *New York Tribune*, Sep 25 1918.

23. "Too many wealthy war loan slackers." *Seattle Star*, Oct 3 1918.

24. "N.Y. district still lags in taking bonds." *Sun* (NY), Oct 5 1918.

25. "Liberty loan slackers to be published." *Chico Record* (CA), Oct 8 1918.

26. "M'Adoo raps rich as loan slackers." *Washington Times*, Oct 12 1918.

Chapter 5.

1. "Chase Liberty loan slackers." *Ardmoreite* (Ardmore OK), Jun 3 1917.

2. "Government inspector here." *Evening Times-Republican* (Marshalltown IA), Oct 30 1917.

3. "Uncle Sam finding out who bond slackers are." *Seattle Star,* Apr 10 1918.

4. "Farmers called loan slackers." *New York Tribune*, Apr 11 1918.

5. "Bond slackers will be reported." *Butler Times* (MO), Apr 11 1918.

6. "Will keep list of bond slackers." *Lake County Times* (Hammond IN), Apr 12 1918.

7. "Los Griegos is interested in big loan drive." *Albuquerque Morning Journal* (NM), Apr 13 1918.

8. "Large cities lagging in drive for loan." *Evening Public Ledger* (Philadelphia), Apr 18 1918.

9. "Seven prove loyalty." *Sunday Oregonian* (Portland), Apr 21 1918.

10. "Use yellow tags." *Topeka State Journal* (KS), Apr 23 1918.

11. "Liberty bond slackers may be exposed thru publicity." *Durant News* (OK), Apr 26 1918.

12. "30,000 bond slacker suspects face quiz." *Sun* (NY), Jun 8 1918.

13. "Government agents are after liberty loan slackers." *Ogden Standard* (UT), Jun 14 1918.

14. "Loan slackers appear." *Ogden Standard* (UT), Jun 17 1918.

15. "W. S. Stamps slackers to be recorded." *Bourbon News* (Paris KY), Jun 25 1918.

16. "Red Cross slackers are being checked." *Glascow Courier* (MT), Mar 29 1918.

17. "Round up Red Cross slackers." *Chickasha Express* (OK), Nov 1 1918; "Roll call campaign

continues." *Chickasha Express* (OK), Dec 31 1918.

18. "Nine slacker cases reported in Boone." *Evening Missourian* (Columbia), Jan 28 1918.

19. "Kansas City liberty loan managers after financial slacker from Tulsa." *Tulsa World,* Apr 10 1918.

20. "Raises some assessments; lowers others." *Evening Times-Republican* (Marshalltown IA),

Oct 3 1918.

21. "Bond slackers come across before committee." *Lake County Times* (Hammond IN), Oct 5 1918;

"Some bond slackers don't show." *Lake County Times* (Hammond IN), Oct 22 1918.

22. "U.S. loan total now $2,269,876,200." *Sun* (NY), Oct 12 1918.

23. "Final drive for liberty loan slackers." *South Bend News-Times* (IN), Oct 13 1918.

24. "Loan slackers may face the Kansas City plan." *Ardmoreite* (Ardmore OK), Oct 16 1918.

25. "Pace is starting to put Phoenix over the top." *Arizona Republican* (Phoenix), Oct 16 1918.

26. "To watch for bond slackers." *Butler Times* (MO), Oct 17 1918.

27. "Slackers are called to account." *Public Ledger* (Maysville KY), Oct 19 1918.

28. "News that city reaches quota." *Seattle Star*, Oct 19 1918.

29. "May have trouble says county atty." *Redwood Gazette* (MN), Nov 6 1918.

30. "Bond slackers in court." *University of North Carolina Newsletter* (Chapel Hill), Nov 13 1918.

31. "Stamp slacker lists proposed. *Oklahoma City Times*, Jan 16 1919.

32. "Defense council will arrest loan slackers, says head." *Great Falls Tribune* (MT), Apr 15 1919.

33. "Bond slackers will be made to explain." *Forest City Press* (SD), Apr 17 1919.

Chapter 6.

1. "Bond workers needed here; may draft 'em." *Oklahoma City Times*, Oct 16 1917.

2. "Printing the names." *Oklahoma City News*, Oct 19, 1917.

3. "He's bond slacker." *Topeka State Journal* (KS), Oct 20 1917.

4. "Bond slackers to be hunted down." *Tulsa World* (OK), Oct 21 1917.

5. "Pull the fangs of the traitors." *Richmond Palladium* (IN), Oct 27 1917.

6. "Shame on Smyre." *Liberal Democrat* (KS), Jan 10 1918.

7. "Loan slackers to have names published." *Journal-Miner* (Prescott AZ), Apr 17 1918.

8. No title. *Aurora Observer* (OR), Apr 18 1918.

9. "Every Oregon city is over the top." *Sunday Oregonian* (Portland), Apr 21 1918.

10. "Link to purchase bond." *Morning Oregonian* (Portland), May 1, 1918.

11. "A. T. Link branded as bond slacker." *Morning Oregonian* (Portland), May 2 1918.

12. "Link buys $100 bond." *Morning Oregonian* (Portland), May 3 1918.

13. "A. T. Link, principal of Link's Business College answers statements." *Sunday Oregonian* (Portland), May 5 1918.

14. "Melton threatens to publish names of bond slackers." *Oklahoma City Times*, May 4 1918.

15. No title. *Liberal Democrat* (KS), May 9 1918.

16. "Third liberty loan committee roasts bond slackers." *Washington Standard* (Olympia), May 10 1918

17. "Liberty bond slackers." *Washington Standard* (Olympia), May 17 1918.

18. "A suggestion." Lynden Tribune (WA), May 23 1918.

19. "Publish thrift stamp slacker list soon." *Chattanooga News* (TN), Jul 8 1918.

20. "Slacker list brings many subscriptions." *Chattanooga News* (TN), Jul 16 1918.

21. "Local comment." *Evening Times-Republican* (Marshalltown IA), Sep 28 1918.

22. Ben Hur Lampman. "Well-to-do fail in buying bonds." *Morning Oregonian* (Portland) Sep 30 1918.

23. Ibid.

24. No title. *East Oregonian* (Pendleton), Oct 1 1918.

25. "Sheridan bank head reported bond slacker." *Oregon City Enterprise*, Oct 4 1918.

26. "No camouflage patriotism." *Chico Record* (CA), Oct 5 1918.

27. "Higby Harris worth $175,000 is bond slacker." *East Oregonian* (Pendleton), Oct 5 1918.

28. "Patriotic League expose bears fruit." *East Oregonian* (Pendleton), Oct 8 1918.

29. "To make public all who buy liberty bonds." *Arizona Republican* (Phoenix), Oct 9 1918.

30. "List non-buyers." *Alma Record* (MI), Oct 10 1918.

31. "G. Poncin and G. E. M. Pratt, dollar slackers." *Seattle Star*, Oct 10 1918.

32. "Public is given names of war loan slackers." *Seattle Star*, Oct 10 1918.

33. "Maricopa must raise million and a half more." *Arizona Republican* (Phoenix), Oct 11 1918.

34. "Saylor buys bonds Mesa man in right." *Arizona Republican* (Phoenix), Oct 13 1918.

35. "Bond slackers to receive publicity." *Phoenix Tribune* (AZ), Oct 12 1918.

36. "Bond slacker." *Seattle Star,* Oct 17 1918.

37. "Don't be a bond slacker." *West Virginian* (Fairmont), Oct 17 1918.

38. "Fred R. Aldrich bond slacker." *La Habra Star* (CA), Oct 18 1918.

39. Ad. *Pullman Herald* (WA), Oct 18 1918.

40. "Try to persuade man to subscribe to liberty loan." *Arizona Republican* (Phoenix), Oct 15 1918.

41. "Need 5,000 men who will each take $200 bond." *Arizona Republican* (Phoenix), Oct 17 1918.

42. "Frank Peterson leaves district." *Arizona Republican* (Phoenix), Oct 18 1918.

43. "Mesa loan committee wires to stop the sale of gas to slacker." *Bisbee Review* (AZ), Oct 19 1918.

44. "Slackers are weeded." *Morning Oregonian* (Portland), Oct 18 1918.

45. "Post eight loan slackers." *Watertown News* (WI), Oct 21, 1918.

46. "State and county news briefs." *Bisbee Review* (AZ), Oct 22 1918.

47. "Loan slackers again warned of exposure." *South Bend News-Times* (IN), Oct 24 1918.

48. "Dr. Evans published as slacker" *Madera Mercury* (CA), Oct 25 1918.

49. "Bond slacker on carpet." *Morning Oregonian* (Portland), Oct 30 1918.

50. "4th liberty loan slackers." *Little Falls Herald* (MN), Nov 1 1918.

51. "Exposing financial slackers." *Evening Times-Republican* (Marshalltown IA), Dec 22 1917.

52. "Fake Hearst fashion writer sued." *Evening Capital News* (Boise ID), Apr 16 1919.

Chapter 7.

1. "Teamster fined three $100 liberty bonds." *Public Ledger* (Maysville KY), Jun 14 1917.

2. "Drumright Red Cross slackers fined in court." *Oklahoma City Times*, Jun 27 1917.

3. "Force German to buy liberty bonds." *Laurens Advertiser* (SC), Oct 31 1917; "Germans in shadow of jail buy bonds." *Sun* (NY), Oct 26 1917.

4. "Iowan sells bonds to escape prison." *Fort Dodge Messenger* (IA), Oct 25 1917.

5. "Banker arrested; loan foe, charged." *Bemidji Pioneer* (MN), Oct 25 1917.

6. "Triumph banker guilty of opposing liberty loan." *Bemidji Pioneer* (MN), Nov 17 1917; "News of the state." *New Ulm Review* (MN), Nov 28 1917.

7. "Third degree routs Teuton sympathizers." *Missoulian* (Missoula MT), Nov 9 1917.

8. "Bond slackers made to dig up." *Evening Times-Republican* (Marshalltown IA), Apr 13 1918.

9. "Action is prompt." *Morning Oregonian* (Portland), Apr 16 1918.

10. "Confesses he was wrong." *St. Johns Review* (OR), Apr 19 1918.

11. Ibid.

12. "Arrest on treason charge is admitted" *Morning Oregonian* (Portland), Oct 22 1918.

13. "Loan slacker is fined." *Morning Oregonian* (Portland), Oct 30, 1918.

14. "Alien money to buy bonds in liberty loan." *Journal-Miner* (Prescott AZ), Apr 17 1918.

15. "No mercy is shown for bond slackers." *Tulsa World* (OK), Apr 12 1918.

16. "7 Socialist aldermen indorse liberty loan." *New York Tribune*, Apr 10 1918.

17. "Alderman Lee is threatened with lynching." *Sun* (NY), Feb 27 1918; "Willful Reds to be curbed

by aldermen." *New York Tribune,* Feb 28 1918.

18. "Loan slacker goes off jury by order." *Arizona Republican* (Phoenix), Apr 19 1918.

19. No title *Copper Era* (Clifton AZ), Apr 19 1918.

20. "A slacker's fate. *Bisbee Review* (AZ), Apr 20, 1918.

21. "Schwamm arrested for violation of Espionage Act." *Tombstone Epitaph* (AZ), Apr 21 1918.

22. "Bond slacker beaten." *Banner* (Cambridge MD), Apr 20 1918.

23. "Tar and feathers for twelve men." *Banner* (Cambridge MD), Apr 20 1918.

24. "S. P. employees run bond slackers out." *East Oregonian* (Pendleton), Apr 20 1918.

25. "Yellow paint." *Madison Leader* (SD), Apr 20 1918.

26. "Las Vegas patriots give alleged Liberty loan slacker jaundiced coat." *Evening Herald*

(Albuquerque NM), Apr 22 1918.

27. "How ore town hits bond slackers." *Lake County Times* (Hammond IN), Apr 22 1918.

28. "Workers punish bond slacker." *Harrisburg Telegraph* (PA), Apr 23 1918.

29. "Tar German farmer." *Topeka State Journal* (KS), Apr 24 1918.

30. "Bond slackers are dipped in oil." *Forest City Press* (SD), Apr 25 1918.

31. "Bond slackers denied charter." *Omaha Bee*, Apr 24 1918.

32. "Convenient religion." *Licking Valley Courier* (West Liberty KY), Apr 25 1918.

33. "Ropes and tar effective." *Alexandria Gazette* (VA), Apr 29 1918.

34. "Liberty bond slackers may be exposed thru publicity." *Durant News* (OK), Apr 26 1918.

35. "Slacker's house painted." *Evening Times-Republican* (Marshalltown IA), Apr 26 1918.

36. "Noose changes his mind." *Alexandria Gazette* (VA), Apr 27 1918.

37. "Bond slacker retracts." *Morning Oregonian* (Portland), Apr 27 1918.

38. "Bond slacker scrouged." *Terre Haute Tribune* (IN), Apr 28 1918.

39. "Rope around his neck, he agrees to buy bond." *Washington Times*, Apr 29 1918.

40. "Defense council deplores acts." *Denison Review* (IA), May 1 1918.

41. "Man jailed." *Los Angeles Herald,* May 2 1918.

42. "Preacher tagged and disciplined." *Evening Times-Republican* (Marshalltown IA), May 2 1918.

43. "Haefner faces court charges." *Ottumwa Courier* (IA), May 3 1918; "Rev. Haefner is acquitted."
Ottumwa Courier (IA), May 14 1918.

44. "Seward kept record good." *Liberal Democrat* (KS), May 2 1918.

45. "Where technicalities don't go" *Bisbee Review* (AZ), May 3 1918.

46. "Rough treatment for loan slackers." *Evening Public Ledger* (Philadelphia), May 4 1918.

47. "Bond slacker fired." *Fulton County News* (McConnellsburg PA), May 9 1918.

48. "Innocent men abused." *Goldfield News* (NV), May 18 1918.

49. "Wealthy bond slacker ostracized, Glenn rancher is given floater." *Chico Record* (CA),

May 19, 1918.

50. No title. *Chico Record* (CA), May 21 1918.

51. "Bank stops dealing with bond slackers." *Grenada Sentinel* (MS), May 31 1918.

52. "Union men will not work with bond slackers." *Santa Cruz Evening News* (CA), Apr 22 1918.

53. "Patriotism acid test in choosing Bisbee officials." *Bisbee Review* (AZ), May 26 1918.

54. "Patriotism acid test in choosing Bisbee officials." *Bisbee Review* (AZ), May 26 1918; "Citizens'

ticket with clean sweep wins three wards." *Bisbee Review* (AZ), May 28 1918.

55. "Red Cross slacker tarred. *Sun* (NY), May 22 1918.

56. "Tar and feathers for four." *Alexandria Gazette* (VA), May 27 1918.

57. "Yellow paint for Red Cross slackers." *Bismarck Tribune* (ND), May 28 1918.

58. "McGill patriots ride Red Cross slacker on a rail." *Elko Independent* (NV), May 29 1918.

59. "Whip, tar and feather a Red Cross slacker." *Liberal Democrat* (KS), May 30 1918.

60. "Red Cross slacker ridden on radiator and rolled in mud." *Bisbee Review* (AZ), Jun 9 1918.

61. "Loan slacker badly beaten." *Sun* (NY), Jun 3 1918.

62. "Man accused." Los Angeles Herald, Jun 18 1918.

63. "Stamp slacker is drenched and painted by shop employees." *Sacramento Union* (CA),
Jun 30 1918.

64. "W. S. S. quarrel ends in shooting." *Copper Era* (Clifton AZ), Jun 28 1918.

65. "Bond slacker repents." *Morning Oregonian* (Portland), Jul 1 1918.

66. "Slackers receiving letters from the committee." *Ogden Standard* (UT), Jul 5 1918.

67. "Stamp slackers few in Keokuk." *Gate City* (Keokuk IA), Aug 14 1918.

68. "Bond slacker fired." *Tribune* (Terre Haute (IN), Sep 27 1918.

69. "Pay or fight is slogan of loyal squad." *Tribune* (Terre Haute IN), Sep 27 1918.

70. "Liberty court to summon all loan slackers." *Rock Island Argus* (IL), Sep 28 1918.

71. Ibid.

72. "Bond slacker is forced to buy bonds." *Ontario Argus* (OR), Oct 3 1918.

73. "Drafting liberty loan slackers." *Evening World* (NY), Oct 4 1918.

74. "Slacker is given ride on liberty long pole." *Oregon City Enterprise*, Oct 4, 1918.

75. "Shasta is after slackers." *Chico Record* (CA), Oct 8 1918.

76. "Force idea not to be countenance by the liberty loan body." *Tulsa World* (OK), Oct 13 1918.

77. "Bond buyers in chorus denounce city's slackers in fourth drive." *Harrisburg Telegraph* (PA),
Oct 14 1918.

78. "Bond slackers." *Harrisburg Telegraph* (PA), Oct 14 1918.

79. "Arizonans are rough with the loan slackers." *El Paso Herald* (TX), Oct 14 1918.

80. "Painted yellow bond slacker is made to parade." *Arizona Republican* (Phoenix), Oct 16 1918.

81. "While in asylum his money taken Charles Reas says." *Arizona Republican* (Phoenix) Oct 17 1918.

82. "Man paraded as bond slacker now in asylum." *Arizona Republican* (Phoenix), Oct 23 1918.

83. "This should be prosecuted." *Arizona Republican* (Phoenix), Oct 24 1918.

84. No title. *Marin Journal* (CA), Oct 17 1918.

85. "Strong Arm Committee on job in McMechen." *Wheeling Intelligencer* (WV), Oct 17 1918.

86. "Liberty loan slacker placarded in Fayette." *Bourbon News* (KY), Oct 18 1918.

87. "Big crowd at mass meeting." *Baxter Springs News* (KS), Oct 18 1918.

88. "Ninety days for bond slacker." *Santa Cruz Evening News* (CA), Oct 19 1918.

89. "The man who doesn't buy." *Farmington Times* (MO), Oct 18 1918.

90. "Bond slackers lose jobs." *Harrisburg Telegraph* (PA), Oct 19 1918.

91. No title. *Riverside Press* (CA), Oct 21 1918.

92. "Bond slacker kills man." *Alexandria Gazette* (VA), Oct 23 1918.

93. "Asks $35,000 damages." *Alexandria Gazette* (VA), Oct 28 1918.

94. "Hard row for bond slackers." *Redwood Gazette* (Redwood Falls, MN), Dec 18 1918.

95. "Loan slackers arrest men for forced purchase." *Richmond Palladium* (IN), Jun 24 1919.

96. "Sue for slacker charges." *Evening Times-Republican* (Marshalltown IA), Oct 23 1920.

97. "Slackers should keep still." *Evening Times-Republican* (Marshalltown IA), Oct 25 1920.

98. "War mothers celebrate bond slacker defeat." *Alaska Empire* (Juneau), Feb 16 1921.

www.ingramcontent.com/pod-product-compliance
Lightning Source LLC
Chambersburg PA
CBHW031951080426
42735CB00007B/352